Language in use
BEGINNER

Classroom Book

ADRIAN DOFF & CHRISTOPHER JONES

Classroom Book Classroom Book Classroom Book Classroom Book Classroom Book Classroom Book Classroom Book Classroom Book Classroom Book Classroom Book Classroom Book Classroom Book Classroom Book Classroom Book Classroom Book

CAMBRIDGE
UNIVERSITY PRESS

PUBLISHED BY THE PRESS SYNDICATE OF THE UNIVERSITY OF CAMBRIDGE
The Pitt Building, Trumpington Street, Cambridge, United Kingdom

CAMBRIDGE UNIVERSITY PRESS
The Edinburgh Building, Cambridge CB2 2RU, UK
40 West 20th Street, New York, NY 10011–4211, USA
477 Williamstown Road, Port Melbourne, VIC 3207, Australia
Ruiz de Alarcón 13, 28014 Madrid, Spain
Dock House, The Waterfront, Cape Town 8001, South Africa

http://www.cambridge.org

First published 1999
Tenth printing 2003

Printed in Italy by G. Canale & C. S.p.A.

ISBN 0 521 62707 9 Classroom Book
ISBN 0 521 62706 0 Self-study Workbook
ISBN 0 521 62705 2 Self-study Workbook with Answer Key
ISBN 0 521 62704 4 Teacher's Book
ISBN 0 521 62703 6 Class Cassette Set
ISBN 0 521 62702 8 Self-study Cassette Set

Contents

Guide to units

	Classroom Book	Self-study Workbook
1 **People and places**	Greetings; introductions; saying where you're from **Grammar:** pronouns; Present tense of *to be*; short forms; *This is …*	Grammar exercises Listening: *Photos*
2 **In the family**	Talking about your family; saying how old people are **Vocabulary:** people; family relationships; singular and plural nouns; numbers 1–20	Vocabulary exercises Listening: *Parents and children*
Study pages A	Focus on … The alphabet **Sounds:** /ɪ/, /e/ and /æ/ **Phrasebook:** Greetings **Consolidation:** Pronouns; *have/has*; *my, your, his, her* Review	Check your progress Phrasebook Writing: *My friend Maria*
3 **To be or not to be?**	Correcting people; asking questions **Grammar:** negative of verb *to be*; *yes/no* questions; questions with *Who, What* and *Where*	Grammar exercises Listening: *Spell the words*
4 **Things around you**	Describing objects; giving and receiving presents; saying where things are **Vocabulary:** colours; parts of a room; everyday objects; place prepositions	Vocabulary exercises Listening: *Birthday presents*
Study pages B	Focus on … Numbers 21–100 **Sounds:** /s/ and /θ/, /z/ and /ð/ **Phrasebook:** Excuse me **Consolidation:** *a* and *an*; *this, that, these, those* Review	Check your progress Phrasebook Writing: *Pictures of people*
5 **There's …**	Describing and asking about places; finding differences **Grammar:** *There is/are*; *some* and *any*; questions with *How many…?*	Grammar exercises Listening: *Language school*
6 **Where you live**	Talking about flats and houses **Vocabulary:** rooms; furniture; things in the home; addresses and telephone numbers	Vocabulary exercises Listening: *Who are you?*
Study pages C	Focus on … Possessives **Sounds:** /ɪ/ and /iː/ **Phrasebook:** Can I have …? **Consolidation:** Singular/plural; *a* and *the*; ordinals Review	Check your progress Phrasebook Writing: *Describing places*

	Classroom Book	Self-study Workbook
7 **Things people do**	Saying what people do and don't do **Grammar:** Present simple tense; 3rd person singular; positive and negative forms	Grammar exercises Listening: *I like ...*
8 **Food and drink**	Saying what you eat and drink; describing dishes; asking for things in restaurants **Vocabulary:** food and drink; things on the table at mealtimes	Vocabulary exercises Listening: *In a restaurant*
Study pages D	**Focus on ...** Telling the time **Sounds:** /e/, /eɪ/ and /aɪ/ **Phrasebook:** On the phone **Consolidation:** Object pronouns; frequency adverbs **Review**	Check your progress Phrasebook Writing: *Breakfast*
9 **Do you ...?**	Asking people about what they do; talking about daily routine **Grammar:** Present simple; *yes/no* questions; *Wh-* questions	Grammar exercises Listening: *When are they together?*
10 **Things people buy**	Shopping at a market; talking about shops; saying where shops are **Vocabulary:** buying and selling; shops; things you can buy in shops; place prepositions	Vocabulary exercises Listening: *Shopping*
Study pages E	**Focus on ...** Days of the week **Sounds:** /h/ **Phrasebook:** What does it mean? **Consolidation:** Weights and measures; *I like* and *I'd like* **Review**	Check your progress Phrasebook Writing: *My top three places*
11 **What's going on?**	Saying what people are doing and where they are; asking what people are doing **Grammar:** Present continuous tense; *yes/no* and *Wh-* questions; place expressions	Grammar exercises Listening: *On the phone*
12 **Describing people**	Saying what people are wearing and what they look like; talking about jobs **Vocabulary:** clothes; jobs and places of work; adjectives for describing people	Vocabulary exercises Listening: *Where are the Browns?*
Study pages F	**Focus on ...** Imperatives **Sounds:** /ɒ/ and /ʌ/ **Phrasebook:** Hurry up! **Consolidation:** Expressions with *have*; *at* + place **Review**	Check your progress Phrasebook Writing: *People doing things*

	Classroom Book	Self-study Workbook
13 How much?	Talking and asking about quantity; asking people for things **Grammar:** count and non-count nouns; *much* and *many*; *some* and *any*; forms of *have got*	**Grammar exercises** Listening: *I want …*
14 Around the year	Talking about seasons, climate and weather **Vocabulary:** words for describing the weather; seasons; months of the year	**Vocabulary exercises** Listening: *Good times, bad times*
Study pages G	**Focus on …** Can **Sounds:** /v/ and /w/ **Phrasebook:** Would you like …? **Consolidation:** *have* and *have got;* numbers over 100; Review	**Check your progress** Phrasebook Writing: *Birthdays*
15 In the past 1	Talking about past actions; telling a story; describing something in the past **Grammar:** Past simple tense; Past tense of the verb *to be*; irregular past forms; past time expressions	**Grammar exercises** Listening: *The next morning*
16 Around the world	Describing countries; talking about languages **Vocabulary:** geographical terms; names of countries and continents; languages	**Vocabulary exercises** Listening: *Other languages*
Study pages H	**Focus on …** Dates **Sounds:** /ʃ/, /tʃ/ and /dʒ/ **Phrasebook:** I'm not sure **Consolidation:** Verbs with two objects; *in* and *on* + place Review	**Check your progress** Phrasebook Writing: *and, so, because*
17 In the past 2	Saying what people did and didn't do; asking questions about the past; remembering **Grammar:** Past simple tense, positive and negative; *yes/no* and *Wh-* questions; more irregular past forms	**Grammar exercises** Listening: *Can you remember?*
18 How to get there	Talking about ways of travelling and moving around; giving directions **Vocabulary:** direction prepositions; public transport; expressions for giving directions	**Vocabulary exercises** Listening: *Bags of gold*
Study pages I	**Focus on …** Short answers **Sounds:** /l/ **Phrasebook:** Let's … **Consolidation:** *very, quite* and *not very*; years Review	**Check your progress** Phrasebook Writing: *Then …*

	Classroom Book	Self-study Workbook
Unit 19 You mustn't do that!	Explaining rules; asking for and giving permission; saying what you have to and don't have to do **Grammar:** *must* and *mustn't*; *can* and *can't*; *have to* and *don't have to*	Grammar exercises Listening: *House rules*
Unit 20 The body	Describing bodies and actions; describing physical appearance; describing actions **Vocabulary:** parts of the body; adjectives describing physical appearance; action verbs	Vocabulary exercises Listening: *Exercises*
Study pages J	**Focus on ...** Adverbs **Sounds:** /r/ **Phrasebook:** Could you ...? **Consolidation:** Verbs with *to, at* and *about* **Review**	Check your progress Phrasebook Writing: *Animals*
Unit 21 Good, better, best	Making comparisons; describing outstanding features **Grammar:** comparative adjectives; *than*; superlative adjectives	Grammar exercises Listening: *Buying things*
Unit 22 Free time	Talking about leisure activities and sport; talking about likes and dislikes **Vocabulary:** leisure activities and sports; leisure facilities; *like/enjoy + -ing*	Vocabulary exercises Listening: *At the weekend*
Study pages K	**Focus on ...** Verb + *to* + infinitive **Sounds:** /ɑː/, /ɔː/, /ɜː/ and /ə/ **Phrasebook:** What did you say? **Consolidation:** Expressions with *go* **Review**	Check your progress Phrasebook Writing: *and, but, also*
Unit 23 Future plans	Talking and asking questions about future plans; talking about future arrangements **Grammar:** *going to*; questions with *going to*; Present continuous tense with future meaning	Grammar exercises Listening: *At the airport*
Unit 24 Feelings	Describing feelings; expressing opinions about films and TV programmes **Vocabulary:** physical feelings; emotions; adjectives describing quality	Vocabulary exercises Listening: *Three stories*

Final review

1 People and places

1 Hello Goodbye

Greetings • I'm • this is

1 Imagine you are at this party. What do you reply?

2 🔲 Sam meets some people at the party. Listen and fill the gaps.

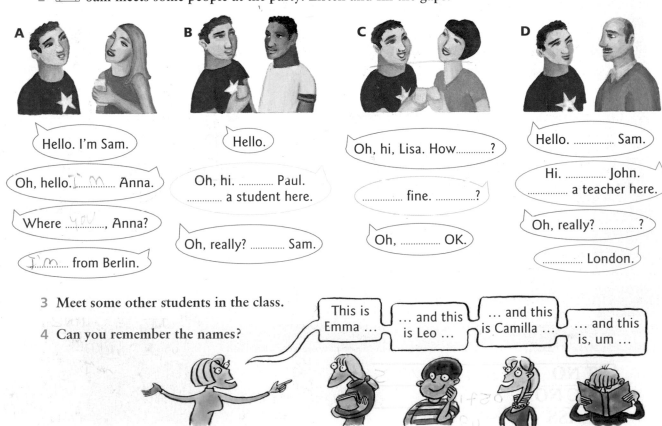

A

Hello. I'm Sam.

Oh, hello. I'm .... Anna.

Where you ...., Anna?

I'm .... from Berlin.

B

Hello.

Oh, hi. .... Paul.
.... a student here.

Oh, really? .... Sam.

C

Oh, hi, Lisa. How ....?

.... fine. ....?

Oh, ... OK.

D

Hello. .... Sam.

Hi. .... John.
.... a teacher here.

Oh, really? ....?

.... London.

3 Meet some other students in the class.

4 Can you remember the names?

This is Emma ... ... and this is Leo ... ... and this is Camilla ... ... and this is, um ...

2 Photos

this is • he's, she's, it's

1 Match the sentences with the photos.

This is my flat.

This is my friend Nina.

This is my friend George.

This is my car.

1 one

2 two

3 three

4 four

Now add other sentences.

He's from London. He's a student.

It's very small.

It's a Citroën. It's very old.

She's from Italy.

2 🔲 Listen and check.

3 Turn to page 104. These are your photos! Make sentences about them.

3 Where are they from?

he's, she's, they're

1 Where are these people from?

A

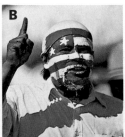
B

C

D

E

F

He's from …

She's from …

They're from …

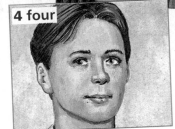

	Australia
	Brazil
	Britain
	France
	Germany
	Italy
	Japan
	Russia
	Spain
	the USA

....

....

....

2 Write more countries in the list.

3 Think of a famous person from a country in the list.
   Do other students know where he/she is from?

Mel Gibson

I don't know.

Tina Turner

Oasis

I think he's from Australia.

She's from the USA.

They're from Britain.

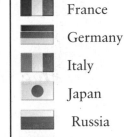

Focus on Form

1 I, you, he, she …

Practise saying the words.

2 I am → I'm

I am	→	I am	→	I'm
You are	→	You are	→	You're
He is	→	He is	→	....
She is	→		→	....
It is	→		→	....
We are	→		→	....
They are	→		→	....

Fill the gaps.

a Hi. .... Michael. What's your name?

b This is Juan and this is Anna. *They're* from Spain.

c This is Lola. *She's* a student.

d This is my car. *It's* very old.

e This is my boyfriend. *He's* from Brazil.

3 Questions

Learn these questions.

> What's your name?

> Where are you from?

> How are you?

How to say it

1 🔲 Listen to these words.

we	you	they
we're	you're	they're
where	how	

Listen to the sentences. Fill the gaps with words from the box.

a ....*How*.... are ....*you*.... ?

b I think ...*is*... students.

c *Where* are ...*you*... from?

d *I'm*.... from the USA.

2 🔲 Notice the stress in these words.

■ .   ■ .   ■ .
London   teacher   student

■ .   . ■ .   ■ . .
Britain   Australia   Italy

Now listen and say these sentences.

. . ■
I'm from London

. . . ■ .
This is my teacher.

. . ■ .
She's a student.

---

2 In the family

1 Families

1 one

2 two

3 three

4 four

5 five

6 six

7 seven

8 eight

9 nine

10 ten

a We have one child.
She's a girl.

b We have three children –
two boys and a girl.

c We have no children, but I
have two cats.

d We have a boy and two girls.
The girls are just babies.

e We're a big family. We have four children – two boys and
two girls. And we have two dogs, a cat and three birds!

1 Five people talk about their families. Read what they say.
Which pictures do they go with?

2 Find words in the texts and complete the table.

3 Look at the other families. Make sentences about them.

4 Work in pairs.

Student A: Choose a family, and make a sentence.
Student B: Which family is it?

> They have
> two babies.

> That's
> picture four.

👤	👥+
a boy	boys
a girl	girls
a dog	dogs
a cat	cats
a bird	birds
a baby	babys
a child	Children

2 How old are they?

1 Look at these birthday cards. What are the numbers?

one
two
three
four
five
six
seven
eight
nine
ten
eleven
twelve
thirteen
fourteen
fifteen
sixteen
seventeen
eighteen
nineteen
twenty

2 Practise the numbers 1–20.

3 Look at the people on page 105. How old do you think they are?

> I think André's nine.

> I think he's ten.

Now listen. How old are they – and where are they from?

3 Parents and children

1 Here are two families. Fill the gaps with words from the box.

mother	father
daughter	son
sister	brother _in_
wife	husband

This is Paul.   1 This is his _wife_.   4 This is her _sister_.

5 This is her _mother_.

2 This is his _son_.   3 This is his _daughter_

This is Isabelle.   6 This is her _father_.

2 Paul and Isabelle talk about their families. Who says these things? Write *I* or *P*.

a [P] I'm married.
b [ ] I'm 19.
c [ ] My daughter is eight.
d [ ] We have two children.
e [ ] My mother's a teacher.

f [ ] I have one brother. His name's Alan.
g [ ] My son is three.
h [ ] My wife is a doctor.
i [ ] I'm a student at university.
j [ ] My father's a taxi driver.

Now listen and check.

3 Write one or two sentences about your family. Read out your sentences.

4 Who's who?

A   **B**   **C**   **D**

1   Look at these four people.

Now read about them. Can you complete the table?

The two women are Alice and Donna.
The two men are James and Bob.

Donna has black hair.
James has blue eyes.

Bob is a waiter.
One man is a student.
The singer has blue eyes.
One person is a police officer.

The police officer is twenty years old.
The waiter is eighteen years old.
One woman is nineteen years old.
One person is seventeen years old.

Alice is from Wales.
The student is from Ireland.
One man is from England.
One person is from Scotland.

The waiter has a green car.
The person from Scotland has a grey car.
One woman has a white car.
One person has a red car.

hair   eyes

red   white   black

grey   green   blue

a singer   a student

a waiter   a police officer

Scotland
Ireland
Wales   England

	Name	Job	How old?	From?	Colour of car?
	Donna	polie officer	19	Scotland	grey
	James Bob	student Waiter	18	Ireland England	green
	Alice	Singer police officer	19	Wales	white
	Bob James	waiter student	18	England Ireland	green

2   Someone does the puzzle. Listen and check your answers.

A Study pages

Focus on ... The alphabet

1 🔊 Listen to these colours.

green   red   grey   blue   white

2 🔊 Listen to the English alphabet.

A B C D E F G H I J

K L M N O P Q R S

T U V W X Y Z

How do you say

– the green letters?
– the red letters?
– the grey letters?
– the blue letters?
– the white letters?

What about the black letters?

3 Ask the teacher to spell the words.

What's number three?

1 there   2 door   3 table

4 chair   5 book   6 fish

7 sun   8 lanp   9 win bow

4 Now test your partner.

 *Spell 'book'.*   *B-O-O-K.*

Sounds: Ten big cats

1 🔊 Listen to these sounds.

/ɪ/   This is my sister.
/e/   Look at the red letters.
/æ/   He has a black cat.

2 🔊 Listen and practise.

children	sister	is	big	picture
	friend	ten	seven	
cats	family	have	has	married	Japan

3 Write a sentence. Use words from the box.

4 Read out your sentence.

Phrasebook: Good morning

Look at the bubbles. Which mean *Hello*? Which mean *Goodbye*?

Good morning.   *Good afternoon.*

Good evening.   *Good night.*

🔊 Listen and practise the conversations.

Consolidation

the woman = she

1 Fill the gaps with *he*, *she*, *it* and *they*.

the girl	=	she	the girls	=	they
Maria	=	....	Maria and Anna	=	....
John	=	....	John and Maria	=	....
my car	=	....	the cars	=	....
London	=	....	London and Paris	=	....

2 Fill the gaps with *is* and *are*.

a My brother .... sixteen.

b Leo and Angela .... married.

c My friends .... at the party.

d My flat .... very small.

e Carla .... from Russia.

f New York and Los Angeles .... in the USA.

have and has

1 All these sentences are in Unit 2. Fill the gaps.

a We .... three children.

b I .... one brother.

c James .... blue eyes.

d Donna .... black hair.

2 When do we use *have* and *has*?

I	We ....
You	You ....
He	They ....
She	

3 Write true sentences about yourself or other people.

My brother has two children.

I have a red car.

My sister has a new bike.

This is my ...

her   your   my   his

Fill the gaps with the right words.

a I have a BMW. ↔ .... car is a BMW.

b Who are you? ↔ What's .... name?

c He has a very ↔ .... car is very old.
old car.

d She's Louisa. ↔ .... name is Louisa.

Review

Questions

Here are some answers. What are the questions?

a – Hi. ....?
– I'm fine, thanks.

b – I'm Bill. ....?
– Oh, I'm Philippa.

c – ....?
– I'm from Madrid.

d – ....?
– I'm thirteen.

Countries

1 Complete these sentences with the name of a country. All the answers are in Unit 1.

a Rio de Janeiro is in ....

b Buckingham Palace is in ....

c Mitsubishi cars are from ....

d Paris is in ....

e The country in the picture is ....

f Berlin and Frankfurt are in ....

g Hollywood is in ....

2 Write a sentence yourself.
Can your partner complete it?

Numbers

1 How do you say these numbers?

7   15   4   11

13   9   12   8   20

2 Look at these numbers. What comes next?

a three, four, five, ...

b nineteen, eighteen, seventeen, ...

c five, ten, fifteen, ...

3 Now test your partner.

3 To be or not to be?

1 Sorry

I'm not, He isn't …

1 Look at the picture. Can you find
   – a baby?   – a waiter?   – a car?
   – a cup of coffee? – a customer?   – a taxi?

2 🖭 Listen to the conversations and complete the sentences.

Conversation A

She isn't ………………………

She's ………………………

Conversation B

He isn't ………………………

He's ………………………

Conversation C

It isn't ………………………

It's ………………………

Conversation D

He isn't ………………………

He's ………………………

Conversation E

They aren't ………………………

They're ………………………

3 Imagine you're in the pictures. What do you say?

Have the conversations.

2 Is this seat free?

1 🔲 **Listen to the dialogue. What are the questions?**
   – Excuse me. ....?
   – Oh. Yes, it is. Thanks. ....?
   – Yes. Yes, I am. My name's Mark.
   – Hi. I'm Sonia.
   – Hi, Sonia. Um, ...?
   – Yes, of course ...

2 **Practise the conversation.**

3 **Look at the bubbles. What are the questions?**

 your book?

 from Ireland?

 a teacher?

 a taxi?

 free?

3 What's this?

1 **Can you answer these questions?**

Who's this?
Where is he?

Who's this?
Where's she from?

Who are these people?

What's this?

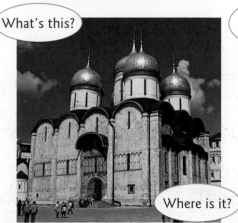
What's this?
Where is it?

What are these?

2 **Look at the pictures on page 104. Ask your partner questions with *Who*, *What* and *Where*.**

Focus on Form

1 I'm not ...

I am not	→	I am not	→	I'm not
You are not	→	You are nøt	→	You aren't
She is not	→	She is nøt	→	She isn't
He is not	→			....
It is not	→			....
We are not	→			....
They are not	→			....

Are these sentences true or false?

a Paris is in Spain.

False. Paris isn't in Spain. It's in France.

b We're in Italy.

c Moscow and St Petersburg are in Russia.

d Toyko and Osaka are in China.

e Bill Clinton is from Brazil.

f This exercise is on page 18.

g This sentence is in German.

Now write a sentence of your own.

2 Yes/no questions

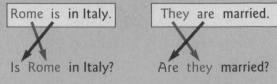

Rome is in Italy.

Is Rome in Italy?

They are married.

Are they married?

Make questions.

a	Peter is a student.	→	.... a student?
b	Her name's Alice.	→	.... Alice?
c	They're from Rio.	→	.... from Rio?
d	Your car is new.	→	.... new?
e	This is your bike.	→	.... your bike?
f	The children are in the car.	→	.... in the car?
g	You're eighteen.	→	.... eighteen?

3 Wh- questions

Make questions.

a	Are you *sixteen*?	→	How old are you?
b	Is he *in London*?	→	Where is he?
c	Is that *Prince Charles*?	→	Who is that?
d	Is your father *45*?	→	How old ....?
e	Are they *in the car*?	→	Where ....?
f	Are those people *your parents*?	→	Who ....?
g	Is her name *Anne*?	→	What ....?
h	Are they *in the café*?	→	...............?
i	Is this *your daughter*?	→	...............?

How to say it

1 🔲 Listen to these phrases and practise saying them.

■ · · ■ · ■
brothers and sisters

■ · ■ · ■
cats and dogs

■ · ■ · ■
London and Paris

■ ■ · ■ · ■
two girls and a boy

2 🔲 Listen to *isn't* and *aren't*. Practise saying the sentences.

· ■ · · ■
He isn't a student.

· ■ · · ■ · ■
They aren't in London.

· ■ · ■ · ■
It isn't my birthday.

· ■ · ■ · ■
They aren't married.

---

4 Things around you

1 Painting by numbers

1 Which colours are in the painting?

red   yellow   black   grey   green

pink   orange   white   brown   blue

2 Work with a partner. Make sentences about the painting. Are they true?

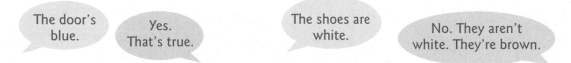

The door's blue.

Yes. That's true.

The shoes are white.

No. They aren't white. They're brown.

3 Now look at these paintings. (They're also on page 105.) What colour is each number?

I think 3 is white.

I think it's blue.

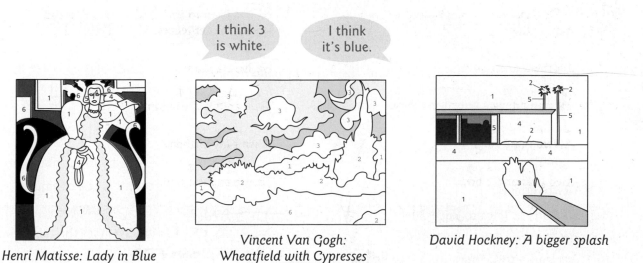

Henri Matisse: Lady in Blue

Vincent Van Gogh:
Wheatfield with Cypresses

David Hockney: A bigger splash

2 Birthday presents

1 Here is a photo of some birthday presents. What do you think they are?

a ring a watch an umbrella a CD a pen a lamp a football a camera an address book a jumper

2 ▭ Now listen. What are the presents?

3 Write down a 'birthday present'. Give it to your partner.

3 Where's my ...?

Where's my watch?

Where are my glasses?

1 Answer the man's questions. Choose expressions from the box.

2 Ask and answer questions about these things.

– umbrella
– shoes
– jumper

3 Work in pairs.

Student A: Turn to page 106.
Student B: Turn to page 108.

Ask and answer questions.

It's ...   They're ...

... on the floor.
... on the desk.
... by the window.
... by the computer.
... in the bag.
... under the table.
... behind the chair.

4 Precious stones

1 Look at these precious stones. What are they called in your language?
Use a dictionary to help you.

amethyst   aquamarine   diamond

sapphire   emerald   ruby

2 Read the descriptions. Fill the blanks.

A ▓▓▓▓▓ are a light blue-green colour (the name means 'sea-water'). Most ▓▓▓▓▓ come from Brazil.

B The best ▓▓▓▓▓ come from South America, especially Colombia. They are green in colour, and very hard.

C ▓▓▓▓▓ are very hard, and also very precious. ▓▓▓▓▓ have almost no colour, but they are sometimes very light yellow, blue or pink. They come from many countries, but especially Australia and South Africa.

D ▓▓▓▓▓ and ▓▓▓▓▓ are actually the same stone. If they are red, they are called ▓▓▓▓▓, and if they are blue they are called ▓▓▓▓▓. Most of them come from India and South-East Asia.

E ▓▓▓▓▓ are a light purple colour. Most of them come from Russia, South America and India.

3 🖭 Someone talks about these four things.
Where are they from? What stones do they have in them?

1 a sword   *2 a brooch*   *3 a necklace*   *4 a bottle*

Study pages

Focus on ... Numbers 21–99

1 Can you guess the missing numbers?

12 twelve	20 twenty
13 thirteen	30 thirty
14 fourteen	40 forty
15 fifteen	50 fifty
16 sixteen	60 ....
17 seventeen	70 ....
18 eighteen	80 ....
19 nineteen	90 ....

2 Look at these. What comes next?

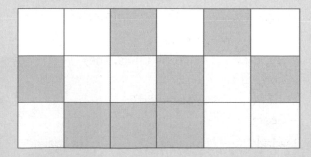

41	42	43	44	45
forty-one	forty-two	forty-three	....	....

3 Say these numbers.

21 **33** 47 56 **62** 78 94

4 Play *Bingo*.

Write ten different numbers (between 1 and 99) in the white squares.

The teacher will read out numbers.

When you hear one of your numbers, cross it out.

Sounds: I think they're sisters

1 Listen to these sounds.

/s/ My sister is a student in France.

/θ/ – You're thirteen. Happy birthday!
– Thank you.

/z/ He's my husband. He's from Brazil.

/ð/ This is my father, and this is my mother.

2 Listen and practise.

Spain	think
office	birthday
student	three

is	mother
has	brother
boys	they

3 Write a sentence. Use words from both boxes.

4 Read out your sentence.

Phrasebook: Excuse me

1 Look at these people. Where are they?

2 Listen to the conversations. Match them with the pictures.

3 Choose one of the pictures. Practise the conversation.

Consolidation

a or an?

a book   a house   an apple   a watch

a cat   a taxi   an ice-cream   a ring

an orange   an egg   an umbrella   a jumper

When do we use *a*? When do we use *an*?

this, that, these and those

This is my brother.   That's my father.

These are my children.   Those are my dogs.

1 When do we use *this* and *these*?
When do we use *that* and *those*?

2 Fill the gaps with *this*, *that*, *these* or *those*.

a Is .... your car?   *b* Look, ... 4 are nice jumpers.   *c* Are .... 3 your glasses?

  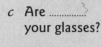

d Is .... seat free?   *e* Look! What's .... 2 ?   *f* Hey! .... 4 are my cigarettes!

Review

Vowels

1 How do you say these letters?

a   *e*   *i*   **o**   *u*

2 Can you read this sentence? What letters are missing?

Y•••r w•tch •s •n th•
t•bl• b•h•nd th• c•mp•t•r.

Male and female

Write the missing words in the table.

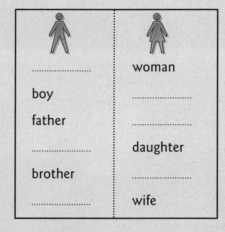

....	woman
boy	....
father	....
....	daughter
brother	....
....	wife

The verb 'to be'

Fill the gaps with words from the box.

am	'm	'm not
are	're	aren't
is	's	isn't

a Excuse me, ...*is*.... this your umbrella?

b – ....*are*.... they from China?
– No, they *aren't* from China. They ....*are*....
from Japan.

c – What ...*'s*... your name?
– George Smith.

d Madrid ....*isn't*....in France. It ....*is*.... in Spain.

e – Where ....*are*.... my glasses?
– They ....*'re*.... on the table.

f – A cup of coffee, please.
– Sorry. I ...*'m not*...a waiter. I ....*an*.... a
customer!

5 There's ...

1 Favourite places

1 Penang, Malaysia

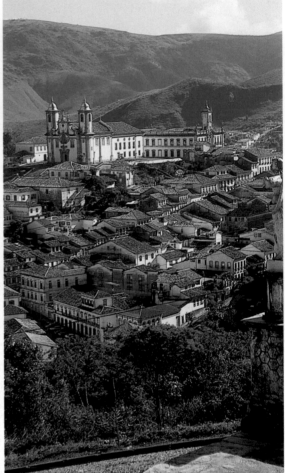

2 Glenelg, Scotland

3 Ouro Preto, Brazil

1 Three people talk about their favourite places. Here are some of the things they say.

Can you match the sentences with the places?

a	1	'There's a very big airport.'	*g*		'There are lots of restaurants.'
b		'There are four or five hotels.'	*h*		'There are mountains all round.'
c		'There are lots of hotels.'	*i*		'There's a church.'
d		'It's a very old town.'	*j*		'There are some beautiful old churches.'
e		'There's just one small shop.'	*k*		'It's a very small village.'
f		'There are lots of tourists.'	*l*		'There are some beautiful beaches.'

▭ Now listen and write *1*, *2* or *3*.

2 Look at the sentences again. What follows *There's ...* ? What follows *There are ...* ?

3 What is your favourite place?
Write two or three sentences about it.

My favourite place is ...

2 Find the differences

there isn't/aren't • some & any

1 Look at the two pictures.

In picture A there's a dog.
In picture B there isn't a dog.

In picture B there are some flowers.
In picture A there aren't any flowers.

Find other differences.
Make sentences with
these words:

– birds
– book
– umbrella
– mountains

2 Can you find any
other differences?

3 Buildings

Questions • How many ...?

1 These people are in the
Empire State Building
in New York.
Can you guess the
answers to their questions?

Is there a restaurant?

Are there any stairs?

How many floors are there?

How many lifts are there?

Are there any shops?

Is there a swimming pool?

How many rooms are there on each floor?

2 Read the text on page 107, and check.

3 Think about the building where you are now.
Ask questions about these things. Do you know the answers?

Is there a ... ?   Are there any ... ?

How many ... are there?

Focus on Form

1 there is & there are

Look at this room.

There's a phone.
There isn't a computer.

There are some flowers.
There aren't any books.

Complete these sentences.

a *There are no* pictures.
b *There is a* lamp.
c *There isn't a* chair.
d *Yes there are* boxes.

2 Yes/no questions

Make questions. What are the answers?

Is there	a computer	
	a lamp	in the room?
Are there	any flowers	
	any pictures	

Look at the pictures on page 107.

Student A: Choose one of the pictures.
Student B: Ask questions. Which picture is it?

3 How many ... are there?

Student A: Look at the street, and ask questions with *How many ...?*

Student B: Look at the street. Then close your book, and answer B's questions.

How many cars are there?

Three.

cars
people
children
buildings
buses
trees
birds

How to say it

1 Listen to the the rhythm of these sentences.

. . ■ . . ■ .
There's a shop in the village.

. . ■ . . ■ .
There are lots of restaurants.

. ■ . ■ .
There isn't an airport.

. . . ■ . .
How many shops are there?

2 Listen to *there* in these phrases.

There's a ...
There are some ...
There isn't a ...
Is there a ...?

Now listen to the sentences, and practise saying them.

There's a phone on the desk.
There are some beautiful beaches.
There isn't a lift.
Is there a toilet here?

6 Where you live

1 From room to room

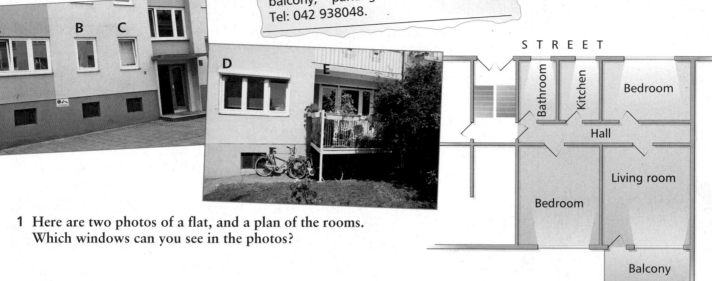

1 Here are two photos of a flat, and a plan of the rooms.
Which windows can you see in the photos?

2 What are the things in the pictures? Match them with the words in the box.

bath	fridge	cupboard
carpet	sofa	single bed
cooker	shower	double bed

Which rooms do you think they're in?

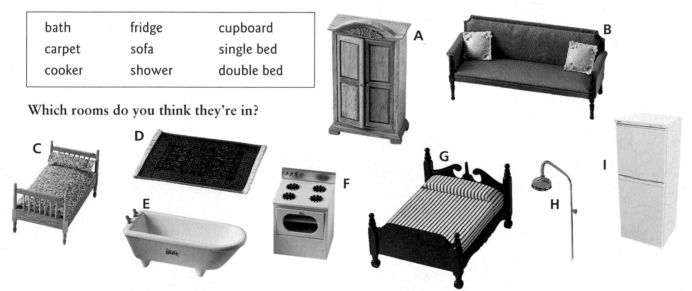

3 🔲 A man comes to see the flat. What rooms does he go into?

What is there in each room?

1. hall – two cupboards
2.

4 Draw a very quick plan of part of your house or flat.

Show it to another student.
Say what there is in the rooms.

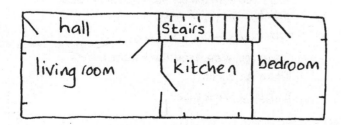

2 There's one in the hall …

1 What do you think these people are talking about?

a 'Well, there's one in the bathroom, of course,
and one in the hall. And there's a big one in
the living room. And there's one in the bedroom,
on the door of the cupboard.'

b 'There are three. There's one on the wall just by
the front door. And there's one on the table
in the living room. And there's one
in the bedroom, just by the bed.'

c 'There are five in the living room, and three
in the kitchen, on a shelf by the window.
And there's a big one on the floor in the
bathroom, and five or six out on the balcony.'

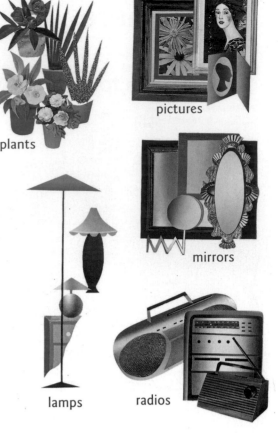

plants

pictures

mirrors

lamps   radios

phones   clocks

2 Think about your own house or flat. Choose one of the objects, and make some notes.

– How many are there?
– Which rooms are they in?
– Where are they in the room?

on the floor?   on the wall?   on a shelf?

by the window?   in the corner?   ....?

3 Talk to other students. Can they guess which object you're talking about?

3 What's your address?

1 Here's part of an address book. Find examples of these things.

country	street	last name
phone number	first name	city
post code		

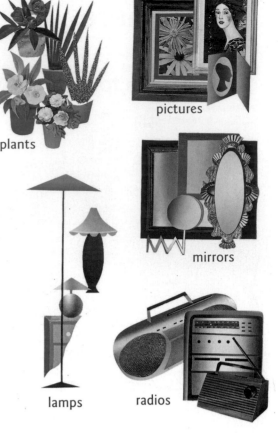

✉ Alison DALEY
Flat 2, 52 New Brighton Road,
Ealing, London W5 9QT
☎ 0181 746 9032

✉ Mario DIMAMBRO
247 Via Napoli, Genova,
Italy
☎ 656631

✉ Philip DENVER
1058 Lincoln Drive,
BOSTON 342354 USA
☎ (001) 617 584 3921

D
E
F
G
H
I
J

2 [cassette] Listen to the three conversations.

There are four mistakes in the
address book. Can you find them?

3 Role-play.

Student A: Tell B your address and phone number. (You can use your
real one or you can make one up.)

Student B: Write down A's address and phone number. Show them to A.
Are there any mistakes?

4 Billionaires

The Sultan of Brunei

These are the two richest people in the world ...

... and these are the places where they live.

Bill Gates

The Istana Nurul Iman, the Sultan of Brunei's Palace

Bill Gates's house near Seattle, USA

1 Read these descriptions. Which do you think are about the Sultan's Palace? And which do you think are about Bill Gates's house?

A There's a big dining room, which has seats for about 100 people.

B It has nearly 1,800 rooms, 18 lifts and about 250 toilets.

C The dining room has seats for 4,000 people – that's a big dinner party!

D In the throne room, the walls are covered in 22-carat gold.

E There are video screens on the walls in all the rooms. These just show pictures – so one day you can have a Picasso, and the next day you can have a Van Gogh.

G If you want to park your car, there's an underground garage with places for about 700 cars.

F There's a library with lots of old books. It also has a notebook by Leonardo da Vinci, which cost more than $30 million.

H The rooms have big windows, so you can see the lake and the mountains.

I It's quite big – it has six bedrooms and about 20 other rooms.

2 Listen and check your answers.

3 Imagine you can spend the weekend at *one* of these places. Which do you choose?

C Study pages

Focus on ... Possessives

1 Read the captions, and complete the table.

I	my
you	your
he	....
she	....
we	....
they	....
Peter	....
my uncle	....

My uncle's car!

This is our flat.

My aunt and uncle, and their baby. Her name is Susie.

My brother Peter on his new bike.

Peter's old bike.

2 Now write captions for this photo.

Sounds: This and these

1 Listen to these sounds.

/ɪ/ The fridge is in the kitchen.

/iː/ Three ice-creams, please.

Listen to the two sounds together.

– Excuse me. Is this seat free?

– His sister's a teacher.

2 Listen and practise.

this is in six pictures kitchen fridge
these three CD
please evening excuse me

3 Write a sentence. Use words from the box.

4 Read out your sentence.

Phrasebook: Can I have ...?

1 Fill the gaps. Use the words in the bubbles.

Here you are

Thank you

please

– Can I have a glass of water, ...?

– Yes, of course. ....

– ....

2 Listen to the conversation.

3 Practise the conversation. You are at a friend's flat. You want:

a cup of coffee   a glass of water   an apple   a banana   a glass of orange juice

Consolidation

Singular and plural

Singular		Plural	
	a tourist		tourists
	a box		boxes
	a baby		babies

Make these words plural.

table	country	boy	beach	university
book	glass	watch	airport	student

a and the

Can I have a paper, please?

Where's the paper?

My father's a teacher. My mother's a teacher too.

Sh! Here's the teacher.

Is there a library in this town?

Sorry – the library's closed.

Choose a or the.

a I have two dogs and *a/the* cat.

b – Where's my umbrella? – It's by *a/the* door.

c My sister's 18. She's *a/the* student.

d I think there's *a/the* bottle of water in *a/the* fridge.

e – Here you are – happy birthday.
 – Oh, it's *a/the* clock! Thanks!

First, second, third …

Look at this building. Can you label floors 6–10?

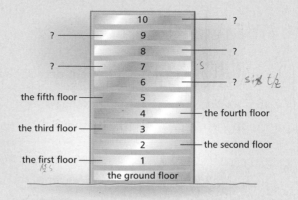

	10	?
?	9	
	8	?
?	7	
	6	?
the fifth floor	5	
	4	the fourth floor
the third floor	3	
	2	the second floor
the first floor	1	
	the ground floor	

Review

Where …?

Ask and answer questions with *Where* …?

Ask about

– the man
– the woman
– the cat
– the children
– the birds.

Vocabulary

Add words to these lists.

a police officer, taxi driver, ...

b orange, pink, blue, ...

c mother, father, daughter, ...

Consonants

1 How do you say these letters?

b d f j l m n p r t w

2 What are the missing letters?

7 Things people do

1 Free time

1 Read about Annabelle Smith. What does she say? Use phrases from the box. *cайfa*

watch television	read a newspaper	have a sandwich	play table tennis
listen to the radio	go to the shops	talk to my friends	look out of the window

Annabelle Smith is from London, England.
She's 22 years old, and she's a computer programmer.

When I'm on a bus …
… I ____ or ____ .
Sometimes I just ____ .

In my lunchbreak …
… I go to a café with some friends, and we ____ .
Then we usually ____ or sometimes I ____ .

When I'm ill in bed …
… I ____ or ____ . And I sleep a lot!

2 Three other people talk about what they do.
What do you think they say? Use the red verbs.

Speaker 1: **When I'm on a bus …**

 *music*
a magazine   *a computer game*

Speaker 2: **In my lunchbreak …**

  football
a burger   *the park*

Speaker 3: **When I'm ill in bed …**

a book   *videos*   *cards*

🔲 **Listen and check your answers.**

3 Choose one of the situations. Say what you do.

---

2 Friends

1 Find opposites in the table. Use a dictionary.

high	weak
cold	long
slow	hot
old	low
short	fast
strong	new

2 Fill the gaps in the poem.

📼 Now listen to the poem.

3 Look at the poem and complete the table.

I like	He ....
I	He wears
I have	He ....

4 Write about a friend or someone in your family.

My sister has long black hair.
She wears jeans. She likes pizza.

Friends

John likes black coffee, I like white.
I like daytime, John likes night.
I like ...hot... showers, he likes cold ones.
I wear new clothes, he wears ...old... ones.

John has ...short... hair, I have long.
I like weak tea, he likes ...strong...
I wear high heels, he wears ...long... ones.
He likes ...fast... cars, I like slow ones.

Why are we friends? Because, you see,
I like him, but he likes me.

3 I don't smoke

1 Which sentences are true of you?
• Write ticks (✓) in the boxes.

Tell your partner your answers.

2 How are you different from your partner?
Tell other students.

She wears glasses. I don't wear glasses.

I drink alcohol. He doesn't drink alcohol.

1	☐ I smoke.	☐ I don't smoke.
2	☐ I eat meat.	☐ I don't eat meat.
3	☐ I play tennis.	☐ I don't play tennis.
4	☐ I wear glasses.	☐ I don't wear glasses.
5	☐ I drink alcohol.	☐ I don't drink alcohol.
6	☐ I play the piano.	☐ I don't play the piano.
7	☐ I speak German.	☐ I don't speak German.

3 Choose someone you all know.
What do you think his/her answers are?
Write down your guesses.

Now find out the answers!

1 She doesn't smoke.
2 She eats meat.
3

Focus on Form

1 Verb + s

I You We They + verb	He She It + verb + s

I speak French.	She speaks French.
You like pizza.	He likes pizza.
We play football.	He ....
They drink coffee.	She ....
My parents live in London.	My father ....

> **Note:**
> have → he has   do → she does
> watch → he watches   go → she goes

Talk about these two people.

I'm Spanish. I live in Valencia. I work in a school. I teach English. At the weekend I play tennis, I read and I watch football.

I'm Spanish. I live in Valencia. I work in a bank. I have a car, but I walk to work. At the weekend I go out with friends and I play tennis.

He …   They …   She …

2 don't & doesn't

I You We They + don't + verb

don't
I smoke → I ̸ smoke → I don't smoke
I drink coffee. → I ....
We like pizza. → We ....

He She It + doesn't + verb

doesn't
He smokes → He ̸ smoke̸ → He doesn't smoke
She speaks French. → She ....
John likes pizza. → John ....

Complete the sentences.

a My boyfriend smokes, but I *don't smoke*
b I speak English, but my parents ....
c My father has a car, but my brother ....
d I like football, but my girlfriend ....
e Dogs like water, but cats ....

> **Note:**
> don't = do n⌀t   doesn't = does n⌀t

How to say it

1 🔲 Listen to the *-s* ending. Practise saying the sentences.

He lives in London.
She has a good car.
She likes pizza.
He smokes a lot.
She wears glasses.
He speaks English.

2 🔲 Listen to the /nt/ sound in *don't* and *doesn't*. Practise saying the sentences.

We don't go to church.
I don't like dogs.
He doesn't smoke.
He doesn't take sugar in coffee.
I don't speak German.
They don't drink beer.

8 Food and drink

1 Food ...

1 Look at the pictures and complete the crossword.
Use a dictionary to help you.

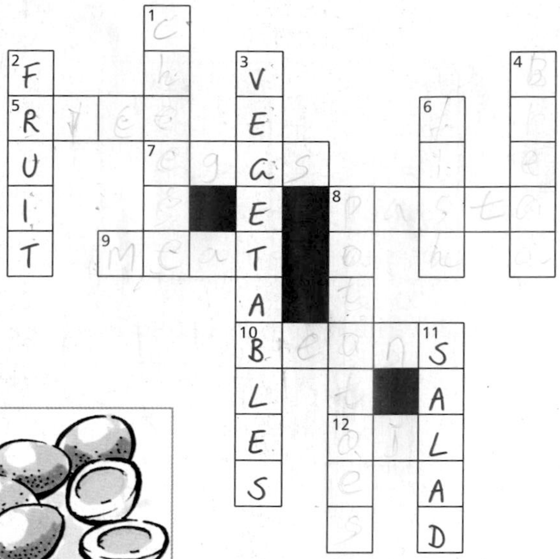

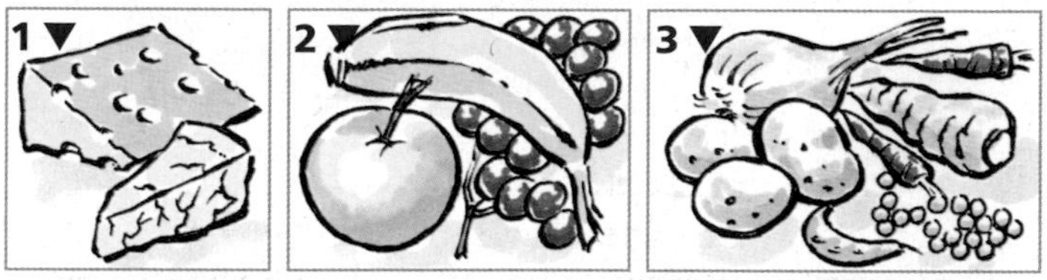

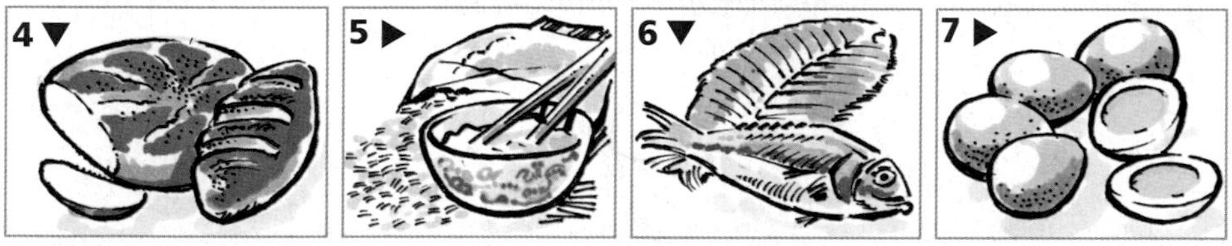

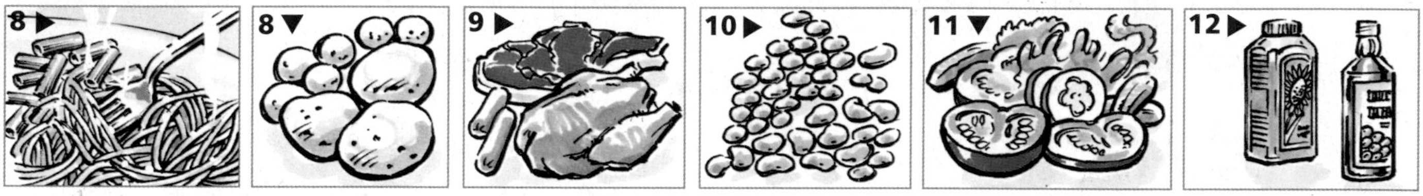

2 Look at these bags of shopping. What food can you see?

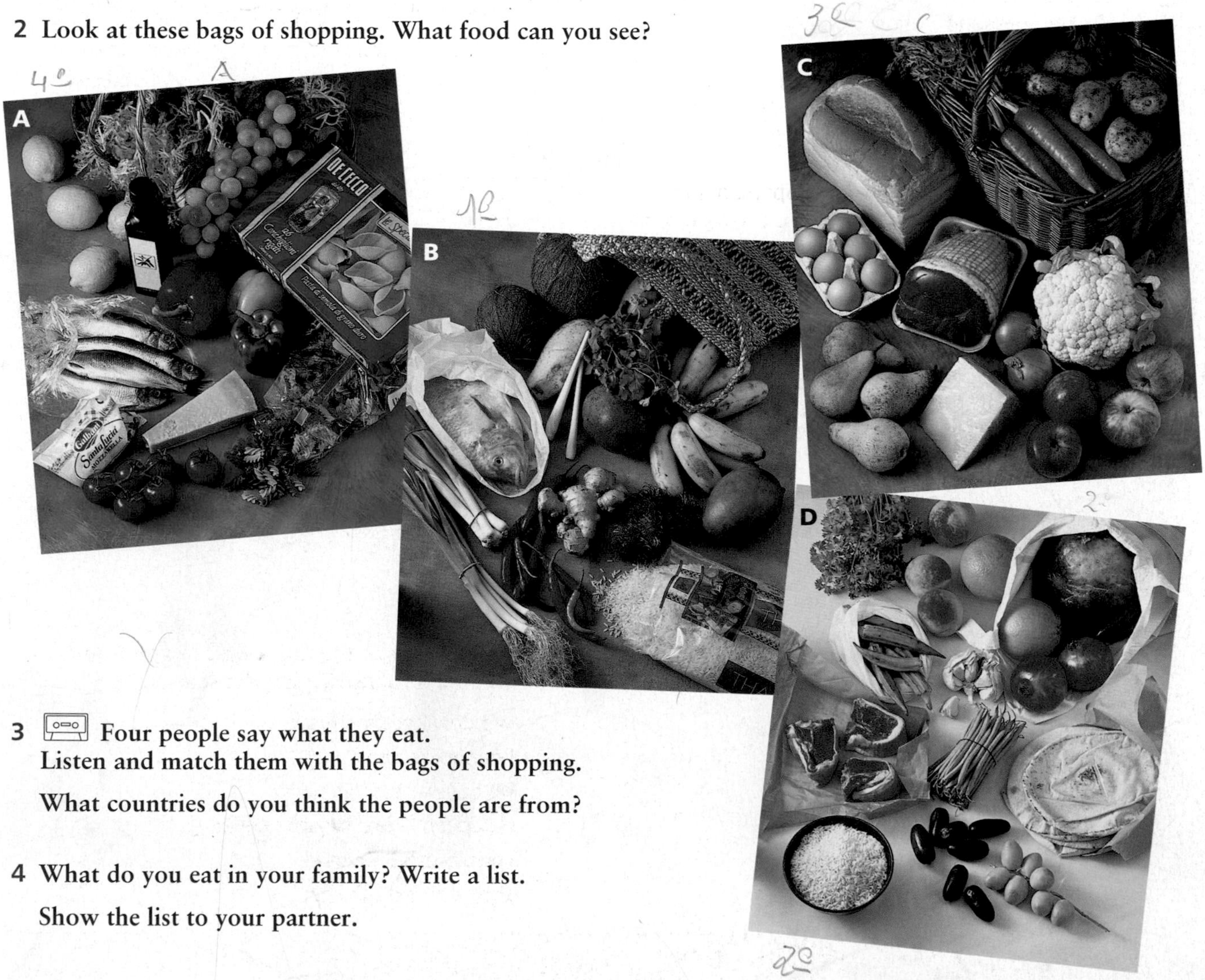

3 [cassette icon] Four people say what they eat.
Listen and match them with the bags of shopping.

What countries do you think the people are from?

4 What do you eat in your family? Write a list.

Show the list to your partner.

2 … and drink

1 Match the drinks with the pictures.

water	milk shake
milk	lemonade
tea	Coca-Cola
coffee	beer
fruit juice	wine

2 Write the drinks in four lists.

LIST 1 I drink this every day.

LIST 2 I often drink this, but not every day.

LIST 3 I sometimes drink this, but not often.

LIST 4 I never drink this.

Show your lists to your partner.

3 Which are the top three drinks in the class?

3 Waiter!

I'm very sorry. Yes, of course.

……………… ……………… , please?

And ……………… ……………… , please.

a plate   a glass

a knife   a fork   a spoon

salt   pepper   sugar   ketchup

1 Listen to the conversation and fill the gaps.

2 Here are three more tables in the restaurant. What do you think the people want?

3 *Role-play*. Work in threes. Have the conversations.

4 Fast food

1 Read the text and find out:

a How many people eat at Burger King every day?

b Which company is the biggest?

c Where do people eat falafel?

d Which company has 200 restaurants in China?

2 Do these companies have a restaurant near you?

THERE'S A *FAST FOOD* RESTAURANT NEAR YOU

Every country has its own kind of fast food – fish and chips in Britain, pizza in Italy, falafel in the Middle East. But some kinds of fast food are everywhere these days.

BURGER KING has around 10,000 restaurants in 56 countries. Every day more than 13 million people eat at a Burger King restaurant .

KENTUCKY FRIED CHICKEN has more than 9,000 restaurants around the world. This includes more than 200 restaurants in China.

PIZZA HUT puts 160 million kilos of cheese on its pizzas every year. There are more than 10,000 Pizza Hut restaurants around the world.

McDONALD'S is the biggest of them all. There are 22,000 McDonald's restaurants in 109 countries – that includes 13,000 in the USA and around 1,500 in Japan. McDonald's cook three million kilos of French fries every day.

That's a lot of restaurants – there's probably one near you.

3 Look at this fast food menu. Do you understand it all?

In a bun

Hamburger	1.20
Cheeseburger	1.40
HOT Chilli Burger	1.60
BIG Burger Bonanza	2.25

In a box

Fish Pieces	1.50
Pizza Slice	1.25
Chicken Nuggets	
6 pieces	1.00
12 pieces	1.80

French fries

Small	0.75
Large	1.30

Children's meals

Hamburger	2.60
Cheeseburger	2.60
Chicken Nuggets	2.60
Pizza Slice	2.60
Fish Pieces	2.60

Desserts

Apple Pie	0.80
with ice-cream	1.20
Ice-cream *vanilla • strawberry • chocolate*	0.80

Cold drinks

Coke, Diet Coke, Sprite, Fanta	
small	0.70
large	1.10
Milk Shakes *vanilla • strawberry • chocolate*	1.20
Orange Juice	1.20

Hot drinks

Tea	0.60
Hot Chocolate	0.95
Coffee	0.95

4 Three customers order food and drink. What do they order? How much do they pay?

5 Imagine you're in the restaurant. What do you order?

D | Study pages

Focus on ... Telling the time

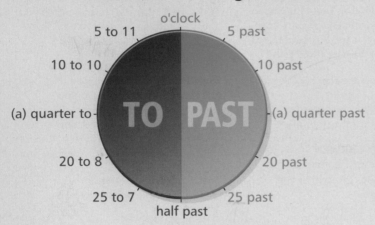

o'clock
5 to 11 · 5 past
10 to 10 · 10 past
(a) quarter to · TO PAST · (a) quarter past
20 to 8 · 20 past
25 to 7 · 25 past
half past

1 Look at the clocks. What's the time?

It's 8 o'clock.   It's half past 4.   It's (a) quarter to 6.   It's 10 past 7.   It's 25 to 11.

It's ....

2 We can also do this:

It's half past four.   `4:30`   It's four thirty.

It's twenty to six.   `5:40`   It's five forty.

What time is it on these clocks?

`7:15`   `11:40`   `2:50`   `12:25`

3 Think of a TV programme you watch. Say when it starts and when it finishes.

I watch Star Trek. It starts at ten past eight and it finishes at nine o'clock.

I watch the news. It starts at six o'clock and it finishes at quarter past six.

Sounds: Bread, cake and wine

1 🔊 Listen to these sounds.

/e/ They eat eggs, vegetables and bread.

/eɪ/ They play table tennis.

/aɪ/ I like rice.

2 🔊 Listen and practise.

> restaurant   bread   vegetables
> table   plate   baby   grey
> wife   I   my   like   white   wine

3 Write a sentence. Use words from the box.

4 Read out your sentence.

Phrasebook: On the phone

Here are two phone conversations.

Fill the gaps. Use the words in the bubbles.

> Can I speak to George
>
> Never mind
>
> Just a moment
>
> Is Louisa there

1 – Hello. Jane Miller.
    – Hello. .... , please?
    – Yes. ....
    – Hello.
    – Hello, George. It's Mike .

2 – Hello. 26439.
    – Hello. .... , please?
    – No, she isn't. Sorry.
    – OK. ....

🔊 Now listen and check.

'Phone' your partner. Ask to speak to a friend.

Consolidation

Subject and object

I like John.   John likes me.

Subject	Object
I	me
you	your
he	him
she	her
it	it
we	us
they	them

Look at these examples, and complete the table.

a – I think she likes you.
– Yes. But I don't like her.

b I sometimes eat potatoes, but I don't like them.

c – Have some coffee.
– No thanks. I don't drink it.

d He talks a lot, but I never listen to him.

e We go to church on Sunday, and my girlfriend sometimes goes with us.

Always, usually, sometimes, never

Mrs Black always goes to church on Sunday morning. She never watches TV.

Jack Green usually plays football on Sunday morning, but he sometimes stays at home.

Mary Grey never goes out on Sunday morning. She usually watches TV.

What do you do on Sunday morning?
Add *always*, *usually*, *sometimes* or *never* to these sentences.

I work.
   I watch TV.
      I go to church.
         I stay at home.
            I visit friends.
               I play football.
                  I …

Review

There is/are

Talk about the town where you live, using *There is(n't)* and *There are(n't)*. Use these ideas:

Rooms

1 Think of the rooms in your flat or house. Where do you

   – wash your hands?   – sleep?
   – have breakfast?   – have a shower?
   – watch TV?   – phone your friends?

2 Which is your favourite room? What's in it? What colours are the things in the room?

More consonants

1 How do you say these letters?

c g h k q s v x y z

2 What are the missing letters in these words?

•nife and for•   •i•t•   •e•ent•   •ue•tion

ma•a•ine   ••ee•e   pi••a   ••ur••

9 Do you …?

1 Men and women

Present simple • Yes/no questions

Here are 10 questions, and answers from 200 people – 100 women and 100 men.
Which do you think are the men's answers, and which are the women's?

Q1 Do you play computer games?

65 _men_ play computer games.

Only 35 _women_ play computer games.

Q2 Do you wear earrings?

Only six ___A___ wear earrings – and five out of the six wear just one earring.

69 _____ wear earrings. Some wear three, four, five and six. One person wears ten.

Q3 Do you sleep on your back?

54 _____ sleep on their back. Most of the others sleep on their side. One sleeps 'in a chair'.

43 _____ sleep on their back. Most of the others sleep on their side.

Q4 Do you like Arnold Schwarzenegger?

24 _____ like Arnold Schwarzenegger. The favourite films are *Terminator I* and *II*.

59 _____ like Arnold Schwarzenegger. The favourite films are *Terminator I* and *II*.

Q5 Do you carry a bag?

95 _____ carry a bag.

69 _____ carry a bag.

Q6 Do you have a pet?

34 _____ have pets. Dogs are the favourite pets. Two people have parrots. One has four dogs and five cats.

51 _____ have pets. Dogs are the favourites, then cats, then fish.

Q7 Do you have sugar in coffee?

47 _____ have sugar in coffee. 30 don't. (The other 23 don't drink coffee.)

62 _____ have sugar in coffee. 24 don't. (The other 14 don't drink coffee.)

Q8 Do you eat at McDonald's?

82 _____ eat at McDonald's. Most of them go 20–30 times a year. One goes every day.

80 _____ eat at McDonald's. Most go 25–50 times a year. One goes every day.

Q9 Do you keep a diary?

24 _____ keep a diary.

Only 16 _____ keep a diary.

Q10 Do you like classical music?

50 _____ like classical music. Mozart and Beethoven are the favourites.

65 _____ like classical music. Mozart, Beethoven and Chopin are the favourites.

1 Read the article, and write *men* or *women* in the gaps.

2 Work in pairs. Ask your partner the questions.

3 Think of some questions of your own.

…… eat ………?   …… drink …………?   …… like ………?   …………………………?

…… have ………?   …… wear …………?   …… play …………?

4 Choose one of the questions, and ask other students. What are the answers?

2 What do you do?

1  Two people meet at a party. Listen to their conversation. How similar are they?

> The woman is … The man is … They both …

2 Complete these questions.

– What ....?
– I'm a student. 学生

– What ....?
– Music.

– Where ....?
– At a school in Cambridge.

– Where ....?
– I live in Cambridge, too.

3 Role-play. Turn to page 107 and choose a role. Write it on a piece of paper.

Imagine you're at the party. Meet two or three other people.
Try to find someone who is similar to you!

3 From morning till night

1 Here are some sentences about a woman's day. Put them in the right order.

a 5 She has lunch.
b 9 She goes to bed.
c 4 She starts work.
d 2 She has breakfast.
e 7 She comes home.
f 3 She goes to work.
g 1 She gets up.
h 8 She has dinner.
i 6 She finishes work.

2 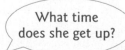 Listen and write the times in the boxes.

3 Work in pairs.
Test your partner.

> What time does she get up?

> At a quarter past seven.

4 Now find out about your partner's day.

Focus on Form

1 Yes/no questions

 They speak English but ...
      ... do they speak French?

 She eats meat but ...
      ... does she eat fish?

 He drinks coffee but ...
      ... does he drink beer?

Add questions.

a They have a dog ...   (cat?)
b He has a radio ...   (television?)
c You play the piano ...   (guitar?)
d She works on Saturdays ...   (Sundays?)
e He likes Mozart ...   (Beethoven?)

2 Short answers

**Look at these questions and short answers.
Which answers are true?**

> Do you
> wear glasses?

> Does your
> teacher wear glasses?

> Yes,
> I do.

> No,
> I don't.

> Yes,
> he/she does.

> No,
> he/she doesn't.

Now answer these questions.

> Do you like
> chocolate?

> Does your teacher
> speak Chinese?

> Does your teacher
> have long hair?

> Do you wear
> high heels?

3 Wh- questions

> Do you study French / Maths / Economics ...?
> → What do you study?
>
> Does he work in a bank / in a supermarket ...?
> → Where does he work?
>
> Does she get up at 7.00 / 7.30 / 8.00 ...?
> → When
>   does she get up?
>   What time

Ask Wh- questions.

a Does she live *in Bangkok / in Budapest* ...?
b Do you work *at home / in a restaurant* ...?
c Does the film start at *5.00 / 6.00 / 7.00* ...?
d Do cats eat *meat / vegetables / salad* ...?
e Does he go to bed at *8.00 / 9.00 / 10.00* ...?
f Do they *watch TV / read* in the evenings?

How to say it

1 🔊 **Listen to *do you, does he, does she*.**

▪ ▪ ▪ ▪ ▪
Do you like him?

▪ ▪ ▪ ▪ ▪
Where do you live?

▪ ▪ ▪ ▪ ▪ ▪
Does he speak English?

▪ ▪ ▪ ▪ ▪ ▪
When does she get up?

2 🔊 **Listen to the /ə/ sound in these
phrases.**

listen to the radio   have a pizza

look out of the window   go to school

Now practise saying these sentences.

I get up at a quarter to five.

I'd like some salt and pepper.

10 Things people buy

1 At the market

1 Look at the market stall. What can you see?

2 Here are three conversations. Put them in the right order.

	Yes, here you are.
	£25.
	How much is it?
	All right, 20 then.
	Oh no, that's too expensive.
1	Can I see that radio?

	I'll have one, please.
	Here you are. That's £1.
	Blue, I think.
	How much are these lighters?
	What colour do you want?
	They're £1 each.

	It's size 38.
	Hello. Can I help you?
	Yes. What size is that jacket?
	Oh, that's too big. Thanks anyway.

🔊 Now listen and check your answers.

3 Choose some other things on the market stall. What questions can you ask about them?

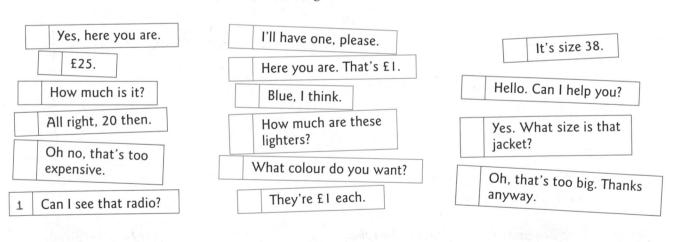

Can I see … ? How much … ? What size … ? … ?

4 Role-play

Student A: You work at the market stall. Sell things to B.
Student B: You're a customer. Buy things from A.

2 Shops

1 Look at the shopping list.
   Which things do you buy at each shop?

2 Think of one other thing you buy at
   each shop. Use a dictionary to help you.

   Together, build up a list on the board.

3 Test your partner.

> Where do
> you buy a jacket?

> At a clothes shop.

Shopping list:

potatoes	1 kilo beef
Time magazine	aspirins
cigarettes	street map
shampoo	apples
pen	T-shirt
sunglasses	chocolate cake

3 Is there a bank near here?

1 Here's part of a town map.
   Where are places A–F on the map?
   Choose sentences from the box.

   It's by the river.
   It's in the next street.
   It's next to the school.
   It's opposite the station.
   It's near the station.
   It's between the school and the cinema.

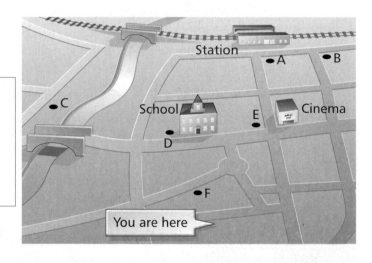

2 Now listen. What are places A–F?
   Where is the bookshop?

 supermarket   bank   post office   restaurant   newsagent   chemist   bookshop

3 Work in pairs.

   Student A: Turn to page 106. Ask and answer questions.
   Student B: Turn to page 108. Ask and answer questions.

4 Think about real places near where you are now.
   Ask and answer questions.

> Is there
> a bank near
> here?

> Yes, there's one
> in the next street,
> opposite the cinema.

4 Open and closed

1 Imagine you're visiting Britain, and you want to answer these questions.

a It's 8.30 in the evening. Where can I buy a bar of chocolate?

b It's Sunday morning. Can I buy bread?

c Where can I buy stamps on a Sunday afternoon?

d It's Saturday afternoon. Can I post a parcel?

e It's 7 o'clock in the evening. Can I buy a pair of jeans?

f It's 4 o'clock in the morning, and I want a magazine. What can I do?

Find answers in the texts.

YOU DON'T FIND KIOSKS in Britain. But there are lots of small newsagents. They sell newspapers and magazines, sweets, cigarettes, drinks and sometimes bread. Nowadays, you can usually buy these things at petrol stations too.

MOST SHOPS are open from 9.00 till 5.30, and they're closed all day on Sundays. But a lot of supermarkets and small food shops stay open later – till 9.00 or 10.00 in the evening, and they're also open on Sundays.

In cities, some supermarkets are open 24 hours a day. Petrol stations also stay open late in the evening, and some stay open all night.

POST OFFICES are open from 9.00 till 5.00 on Monday–Friday, and from 9.00 till 12.00 on Saturdays. But you can also buy stamps in newsagents, supermarkets and petrol stations.

2 🔲 Three people talk about shopping times in three countries. Listen and fill the gaps.

In Poland the banks are open till .... And in towns, supermarkets stay open .... , so you can buy bread ....

In Greece the shops close .... and open again .... But there are also .... , and they stay open all day.

In Thailand many towns have .... You can buy .... there. They stay open ....

3 Think about your own country. When are shops open and closed?

Focus on ... Days of the week

1 [cassette] Listen to the days of the week.

| Monday |
| Tuesday |
| Wednesday |
| Thursday |
| Friday |
| Saturday |
| Sunday |

Practise saying them.

2 Work in pairs. Test your partner.

> Thursday, Friday ...?

> What's the second day of the week?

> Saturday.

> Tuesday.

3 Look at this table. What does the person do?

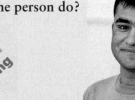

	morning	afternoon	evening	
Mon		✓		I go to the supermarket.
Tues				
Wed			✓	I play table tennis.
Thurs				
Fri			✓	I wash my hair.
Sat	✓			I get up late!
Sun		✓		I go to a football match.

> He goes to the supermarket on Monday afternoon.

4 Think about your own week. Tell other students what you do on different days.

5 Cover up the days of the week. Do you remember how to say them?

Sounds: Hello!

1 [cassette] Listen to the sound /h/ in English. Is it the same in your language?

/h/ Hello. Can I help you?

How much are they?

It's behind the door.

2 [cassette] Listen and practise.

| they have   gets home   half past four |
| her husband   how much   in a hotel |
| at home   his brother   behind the door |

3 Write a sentence. Use phrases from the box.

4 Read out your sentence.

Phrasebook: What does it mean?

Look at the bubbles. Match the questions and the answers.

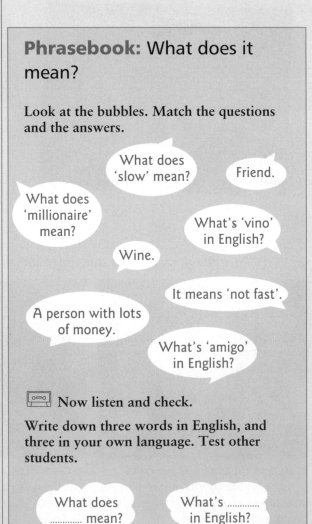

> What does 'slow' mean?

> Friend.

> What does 'millionaire' mean?

> What's 'vino' in English?

> Wine.

> A person with lots of money.

> It means 'not fast'.

> What's 'amigo' in English?

[cassette] Now listen and check.

Write down three words in English, and three in your own language. Test other students.

> What does .... mean?

> What's .... in English?

Consolidation

A kilo of apples

1 A man goes into this shop and buys

  – a kilo of apples
  – four kilos of potatoes
  – 200 grams of beef
  – a litre of mineral water
  – half a litre of milk

  How much money does he spend?

2 Work in pairs. You're in the shop.

  Student A: Buy something from B.
  Student B: Say how much it is.

  > Half a kilo of beef, please.

  > That's five dollars.

I'd like …

I like books.

I'd like this book, please.

I like books =
I think books are good.

I'd like this book =
I want it.

Buy one thing from each shop.

> I'd like …, please.

KIOSK

NEWSAGENT

BOOKSHOP

CLOTHES SHOP

Review

Adjectives

1 Find seven pairs of opposites. Which *three* words are not used?

beautiful	big	short	high
weak	fast	strong	young
expensive	small	rich	long
hot	low	old	cold	slow

2 Choose adjectives to describe things in the picture.

Which word?

Choose the right words.

a I'd like *a/an* orange juice and *a/an* cup of coffee, please.

b My flat has *a/the* balcony. On *a/the* balcony there's *a/the* big sofa.

c – Look at *this/these* jeans. Do you like them?
  – Yes. And I like *this/these* jumper, too.

d I live in *that/those* house over there, behind *that/those* trees.

e There are *some/any* good shops in this town, but there aren't *some/any* good restaurants.

Words

1 What are a–g?

2 What do you use to

  – keep food cold?   – go up to the next floor?
  – cook food?   – find out the time?
  – eat a meal?   – find out the news?
  – look at yourself?

11 What's going on?

1 Windows

Present continuous

He's washing the dishes.

They're dancing.

He's reading the paper.

She's cleaning her teeth.

She's cooking a meal.

He's playing the piano.

They're having dinner.

She's writing a letter.

He's listening to the radio.

He's having a shower.

They're watching TV.

He's making coffee.

1 Look at the windows. What do you think the people are doing? Choose from the list.

🔲 Now listen. Were you right?

2 What are these people doing?

3 Think of an action, and write it on a piece of paper. Mime the action. Can other students guess what you're doing?

I'm playing chess.

I'm making a cake.

I'm washing my hair.

2 Questions

1 ▭ Listen to the conversation.
What are the man's questions?

– ....?

– Er, no.

– ....?

– Yes. Yes, I am.

– ....?

– Excuse me.

– ....?

Practise the conversation.

2 **Look at these answers. What do you think the questions are?**

3 Can I speak to Lisa, please?

Saying where people are

1 **On which days is Lisa**

– at home?
– not at home?

2 **Think of three people you know. Write down their names, and give the list to your partner.**

Student A: Phone and ask to speak to someone on the list.
Student B: Say where they are / what they're doing.

Focus on Form

1 Verb + -ing

Group A		
play → playing	do →	
read →	drink →	
Group B		
writé → writing	have →	
smoké → smoking	dance →	
Group C		
get → tt → getting		
run → nn → running		
swim →		

Add *-ing* to these verbs.

make	go	wash	live	sit	look

2 Present continuous

am / is / are + verb + -ing

Complete the text. Use the Present continuous.

It's Saturday night. The hotel guests (have) a good time. Some people (have) dinner in the restaurant. In the bar, a band (play) slow music. Some guests (sit) at the tables, and others (dance). In the next room, a few people (play) roulette.

In front of the hotel, a man (sit) in a car. He (smoke) a cigarette and he (look) at his watch.
It's two minutes to twelve …

3 Questions

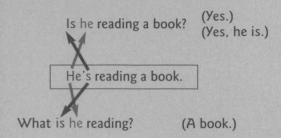

Is he reading a book?   (Yes.)
                        (Yes, he is.)

He's reading a book.

What is he reading?   (A book.)

Make questions. What are the answers?

a She's watching TV. → *Is she watching* TV?
    → What *is she watching?*

b They're going home. → *Are they going* home?
    → Where *are they going?*

c He's making coffee. → *Is he making coffee?*
    → what *is he making?*

How to say it

1 🔲 Listen to the *s* in these sentences. Practise saying them.

She's asleep.

He's at school.

She's away for the weekend.

He's doing his homework.

She's wearing glasses.

2 🔲 Listen to the rhythm of these questions. Practise saying them.

■ . ■.
What's he doing?

■ . ■.
What's she doing?

■ . . ■.
What are you doing?

■ . ■.
What's she wearing?

■ . . ■.
Where are they going?

12 Describing people

1 Clothes

1 Look at these clothes.
   Which do you think are

   – for a woman?
   – for a man?
   – for either a woman or a man?

   Make three lists.

   Show your list to other
   students. Do they agree?

2 Choose a student in the class. Say what he/she is wearing.

   Can other students guess who you're talking about?

jacket

trousers

suit

hat   tie   coat

blouse

shirt

T-shirt

jumper

skirt

shorts

jeans

dress

> This person's wearing a dark green blouse and blue jeans.

> I think that's ...

3 Look at these people. What do
   you think they're wearing?

A

B

C

D

E

2 Jobs

1 Seven people talk about their jobs. Fill the gaps with jobs from the box.

a doctor
an engineer
a singer
a secretary
a shop assistant
a student
a waiter

a I'm ....
I study French.

b I'm ....
I work in a bookshop.

c I'm ....
I sing in a band.

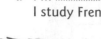

d I'm .... I work
in a Thai restaurant.

e I'm .... I work
in a large hospital.

f I'm .... I work
for British Telecom.

g I'm .... I work for
an insurance company.

2 Three of the people wear these clothes to work. Which people do you think they are?

1

2

3

Now listen and check.

3 Talk about someone in your family.
Use a dictionary to help you.

He
She works in …

He's
She's …

He
She works for …

He
She usually wears …

3 Who do you mean?

tall	hair	
long	fair	grey
short	dark	

1 Make sentences about the people at the bus stop.

He's
She's …

He
She has …

2 Three people describe a woman. What do they say about her?

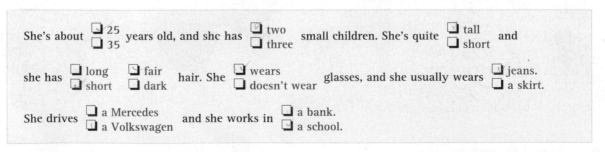

She's about ☑ 25 / ☐ 35 years old, and she has ☑ two / ☐ three small children. She's quite ☑ tall / ☐ short and

she has ☐ long / ☑ short ☑ fair / ☐ dark hair. She ☑ wears / ☐ doesn't wear glasses, and she usually wears ☑ jeans. / ☐ a skirt.

She drives ☐ a Mercedes / ☑ a Volkswagen and she works in ☐ a bank. / ☑ a school.

3 Look at the pictures on page 106. Which is the woman? How do you know?

4 Think of someone your partner knows (e.g. another student, a teacher, a friend, someone on TV). Write three sentences about him or her.

Does your partner know who you mean?

4 Love is all around

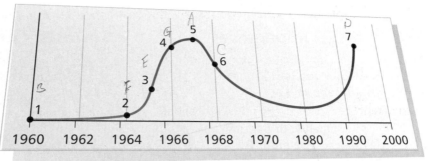

1960 1962 1964 1966 1968 1970 1980 1990 2000

1 Read the story of the 1960s rock singer Reg Presley. Put the seven paragraphs in the right order.

A

A year later, they go back to Larry Page, and he gives them a contract.
Their second song, *Wild thing*, is a big hit, and suddenly the Troggs are rock stars!

CONTRACT

B

Reginald Ball leaves school at 16 and gets a job as a builder. He wants to be a singer in a rock band.

C

The Troggs leave Larry Page. They don't have any more hits. They play in clubs, but they aren't big stars any more.

D

The band Wet Wet Wet make a new version of *Love is all around* for the film *Four Weddings and a Funeral*. The song sells five million copies, and suddenly Reg Presley is a millionaire.

E

Reg Presley writes their next hit – *With a girl like you* – which gets to Number 1 in Britain. In the next two years, Reg writes three more hit songs for the Troggs. One is called *Love is all around.*

F

He starts a rock band with three friends. They call the band 'The Troggs'. Reginald Ball changes his name to Reg Presley.

G

The Troggs make a tape of their songs. They send the tape to producer Larry Page in London. Page likes the songs, but he's very busy. He tells them 'Come back in a year.'

2 Here are four lines of the song *Love is all around*. Can you match the first and second parts of each line?

 Now listen and check.

I feel it in my fingers, … ƒ
Well, love is all around me, …з
It's written on the wind, …з
So if you really love me, …

з… it's everywhere I go
c… come on and let it show
з… and so the feeling grows
ƒ… I feel it in my toes

F | Study pages

Focus on ... Imperatives

1 Listen to your teacher.
Do what he/she says!

> Open your bag and give me £10

Now it's your turn. Tell other students to do things.

Give ...   Open ...

Look at ...   Put ...

Close ...   Take ...   .

2 Look at these examples.

Look!

Don't look!

Drink that.

Don't drink that!

3 Now look at these sentences. Which are correct? Write ✓ or add *Don't*.

How to have a **healthy** life

✓	get lots of exercise.
Don't	smoke.
	eat sweets.
	drink alcohol.
	eat lots of fat.
	eat lots of fruit and vegetables.
	walk to work or school.
	eat late in the evening.
	relax.

Sounds: Coffee on Sunday

1 🔊 Listen to these sounds.

/ɒ/ Do you want coffee?
     The shop's opposite my office.

/ʌ/ That jumper's a lovely colour.
     Are you coming on Sunday or Monday?

2 🔊 Listen and practise.

doctor watch long shop opposite orange hot o'clock	brother colour lovely how much jumper umbrella Monday

3 Write a sentence. Use words from both boxes.

4 Read out your sentence.

Phrasebook: Hurry up!

Match these expressions with the pictures.

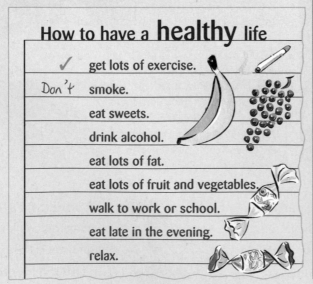

Hurry up!
Sit down.
Wait a minute.
Come in!
Be quiet.

🔊 Listen and check. Practise saying the expressions.

Consolidation

Expressions with 'have'

1 We often use *have* to talk about food or drink.

have breakfast

have a sandwich

have a cup of coffee

We also say:

have a bath

have a shower

have a party

2 Ask your partner:

> When do you have breakfast? lunch? dinner?

> What do you have for breakfast?

> If you go to a café, what do you usually have?

> When do you have a shower? a bath?

at …

1 Notice these expressions.

> She's at home, at work, at school, at a friend's house.
>
> I usually eat at Dino's Restaurant.
>
> You can buy it at the market, at a chemist's, at The Book Centre.

2 Answer these questions.

> Where can I get a drink near here?

> Where can I buy some stamps?

> Where can I get a cheap meal near here?

> Where can I buy a pair of jeans?

3 Think about people in your family. Where are they at the moment?

Review

Present simple tense

Choose verbs from the boxes and fill the gaps.

a My girlfriend and I are both students. I [____] French and she [____] maths. She [____] a room at the university, but I [____] at home with my parents.

| live |
| study |
| have |

b I *(not)* [____] wine, but if it's very hot I sometimes [____] a glass of beer.

| have |
| like |

c My brother [____] in a fast food restaurant. He [____] about 50 burgers an hour. The funny thing is, he's a vegetarian – he *(not)* [____] meat.

| eat |
| work |
| make |

d What time *(you)* [____] in the morning? *(you)* [____] a big breakfast?

| get up |
| have |

e How many languages *(he)* [____]? I know he [____] French, but *(he)* [____] Italian?

| speak |

me, my …

Make pairs and write them in the right diagrams.

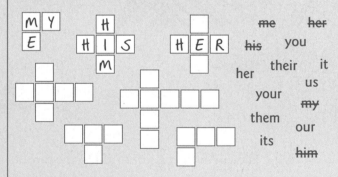

~~me~~   ~~her~~
~~his~~   you
her   their   it
us
your
~~my~~
them   our
its   ~~him~~

Mixed-up words

1 Look at these mixed-up words. Can you make

- three things to eat?
- three shops?
- three countries?

How do you spell them?

CEHIMST   FIRTU

ABEKR   ABILRZ

AANJP   AOOPTT

BCEHRTU

CEEEHS   AEGMNRY

2 Now you write a mixed-up word. Show it to your partner.

ENTIHKC (This is a room)

13 How much?

1 Useful things

Count & non-count nouns • a & some

~~bowl~~	
~~bread~~	
coffee	
cup	
~~eggs~~	
envelope	
flour	
flowers	
keys	
knife	
~~matches~~	
money	
paper	
~~pen~~	
soap	
radio	
shampoo	
spoon	
stamps	
~~water~~	

There's …
a bowl
a pen
…

There are …
some eggs
some matches
…

There's …
some bread
some water
…

1 **What is there in the picture? Add to the three lists. Use words from the box.**

   What is the difference between the three lists?

2 **Cover the picture. How many things can you remember?**

   There's a …   There are some …   There's some …

3 **Work with a partner. You want to**

   – light a fire
   – write a letter
   – make a cake
   – make some coffee.

   What do you need? Write four lists.

   Show your lists to other students. Do they have the same things?

2 Shopping list

lots of • not many/much • not any

1  Two people are making a shopping list. Which of these things do they need? Write them on the shopping list.

tomatoes	rice	bananas
eggs	potatoes	coffee
bread	apples	sugar

shopping list
orange juice

2 Listen again and complete these sentences.

They've got lots of *bread*
They haven't got many *potatoes*
They haven't got much *sugar*
They haven't got any *coffee*

3 Do you know what you've got in your own kitchen? Talk about the things in the list.

We've got some …

We haven't got any …

We've got lots of …

We haven't got many/much …

3 How much …?

How many …? • How much …?

1 Here are four quiz questions. Can you guess the answers?

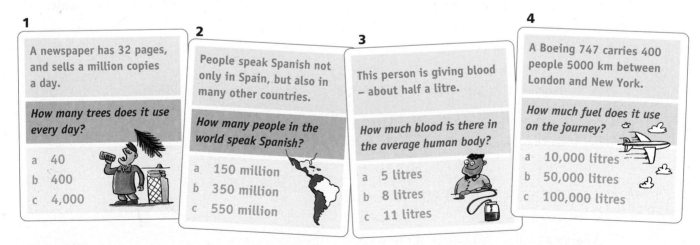

1
A newspaper has 32 pages, and sells a million copies a day.

How many trees does it use every day?

a 40
b 400
c 4,000

2
People speak Spanish not only in Spain, but also in many other countries.

How many people in the world speak Spanish?

a 150 million
b 350 million
c 550 million

3
This person is giving blood – about half a litre.

How much blood is there in the average human body?

a 5 litres
b 8 litres
c 11 litres

4
A Boeing 747 carries 400 people 5000 km between London and New York.

How much fuel does it use on the journey?

a 10,000 litres
b 50,000 litres
c 100,000 litres

What's the difference between the red questions and the blue questions?

2 Make questions with *How many …?* and *How much …?* Do you know the answers?

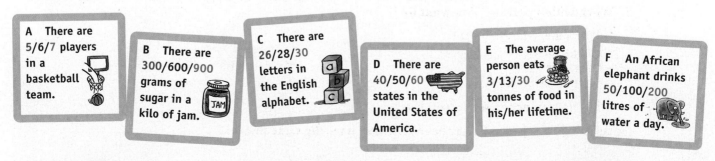

A There are 5/6/7 players in a basketball team.

B There are 300/600/900 grams of sugar in a kilo of jam.

C There are 26/28/30 letters in the English alphabet.

D There are 40/50/60 states in the United States of America.

E The average person eats 3/13/30 tonnes of food in his/her lifetime.

F An African elephant drinks 50/100/200 litres of water a day.

Focus on Form

1 Count & non-count

Count nouns

a boy   two boys   a cup   three cups

Non-count nouns

sugar   a kilo   water   two glasses
of sugar   of water

Count or non-count?

shirt   beef   wine   ketchup
picture   lake   oil   cigarette

2 many & much

Count nouns	Non-count nouns
There aren't many cups.	There isn't much salt.
How many cups are there?	How much salt is there?

Fill the gaps with *much* or *many*.

a How .... wine do we need?

b I don't eat .... white bread, but I eat a lot of brown bread.

c How .... cigarettes do you smoke a day?

d How .... sugar is there?

e They've got a lot of books in their house, but not .... pictures.

f I haven't got .... money in the bank.

3 have got

have		*have got*
I have a bike.	↔	I've got a bike.
I don't have a car.	↔	I haven't got a car.
My sister has a car.	↔	My sister's got a car.
She doesn't have a bike.	↔	She hasn't got a bike.

> I've got = I have got   He's got = He has got

Read out this paragraph using *have got*.

> My brother and I are very different. He has dark hair and black eyes; I have fair hair and green eyes. He has a flat in the city centre; I have a small house in the country. He has a fast car, but he doesn't have any children. I have three children, but I don't have a car. He doesn't have any problems. And I don't have any money.

Think of a person in your family. How are you different? Make sentences with *have got*. Think about these things.

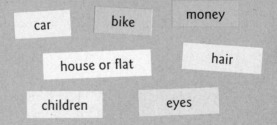

car   bike   money   house or flat   hair   children   eyes

How to say it

1 🔊 **Listen to *'ve got* and *haven't got* in these sentences. Practise saying them.**

I've got a new bike.

I've got brown hair.

We've got some money.

We haven't got much sugar.

I haven't got a car.

2 🔊 **Listen to the /ə/ sound in these phrases. Practise saying them.**

a kilo of rice

a litre of milk

a glass of water

a bag of sugar

a bottle of wine

14 Around the year

1 Seasons

1 Here are four places from around the world.
Which places are

– always hot?
– very cold in the winter?
– dry in August?

Read the texts and find out.

In the summer, Istanbul is quite hot, about 25–30°, and in the winter it is cool. It often rains in the autumn and winter, and it sometimes snows.

Alice Springs is hot and dry all year round. From October to March it is very hot, often 40° or more. From May to August it is clear and warm by day, but cool at night.

Moscow has hot and mainly dry weather in the summer, with temperatures of 25–30°. In the winter it is very cold, and it snows a lot. Temperatures can be below –20°, and there is often snow from November to March. Spring comes late in Moscow, usually in April or May.

Jakarta is hot all year round, and the temperature is about the same in January and July. November to April is the wet season, and in January there is a lot of rain. From July to September it is mainly dry, but the air is always humid.

2 Find pairs of opposites in the texts. Make a list.

COLD

SUMMER

HOT

WINTER

3 Write a few sentences about the weather in your own country around the year.

2 January, February …

1 What are the missing months? Find them in Exercise 14.1 and write them in the table.

2 What month is your birthday? What about other people in the class? Which month has the most birthdays?

3 These two lists are about months in Britain. Which months do you think they are?

> dark nights
> cold
> jumpers and coats
> TV
> Christmas

> school finishes
> swimming
> holidays
> ice-cream
> shorts

Now you choose a month and write a list.

Read out your list. Can other students guess the month?

January
February
June
December

3 What's the weather like?

1 These four people are talking about the weather. Here are some of the things they say. Match the sentences with the pictures.

a ☐ It's cloudy. f ☐ It's hot and humid.

b ☐ It's very windy. g ☐ It's quite warm.

c ☐ It's sunny. h ☐ It's quite cool.

d ☐ It's raining. i ☐ It's very cold.

e ☐ It's snowing.

🔊 Listen and check your answers.

2 Look out of the window. What's the weather like?

3 Guess what the weather's like today in these places.

Weather around the world

Athens	19	rain
	36	sunny

London   Singapore   Moscow   Rio de Janeiro

Get a newspaper and find out!

---

4 Festivals

1 Read about these festivals. Which festivals do the pictures show?

SNOW FESTIVAL (February – Sapporo, Japan)
At the Sapporo Snow Festival people make statues from snow. Some of the statues are *very* big. You can just look at the statues – or you can make one yourself.

CARNIVAL (February – Brazil)
People celebrate Carnival in many countries, but the best known is in Brazil. In Rio de Janeiro, many thousands of people parade through the streets. They wear fantastic costumes and dance to samba music.

HOLI (March – India)
This is a Hindu festival. On the last day of the festival, people sell coloured powder in the street. You can buy the powder, and throw it over other people.

SONGKRAN (April – Thailand)
Songkran – the Water Festival – is the Thai New Year. If you're in Thailand during Songkran, keep your car windows closed, because everyone throws water at everyone.

GIOCO DEL CALCIO (June – Florence, Italy)
This is a 16th-century version of a football match. There are four teams, each with 27 players. The players wear 16th-century costumes. The game is quite dangerous, because there aren't many rules.

OKTOBERFEST (September! – Munich, Germany)
If you like beer, this is the festival for you. Seven million people visit the Oktoberfest. They drink five million litres of beer, and eat a million sausages and half a million chickens.

NEW YEAR'S EVE (end of December)
In most parts of the world, December 31 is the last day of the year. People go out with their families and friends, and at 12.00 midnight, everyone says 'Happy New Year'.

A
B
C
D
E
F
G

2 🔲 **Five people say what they do on New Year's Eve.**

Which things does each speaker do? Choose from the list.

a stay at home
b watch TV
c go to a party
d go to bed early
e visit friends
f go to a restaurant
g go out into the street
h dance
i watch fireworks

3 What do you do on New Year's Eve?

Focus on ... Can

Look! I can swim!

Help! I can't swim!

She can ride a horse.   He can't ride a horse.

They can ski.   They can't ski.

1 Look at the examples and complete the table.

✓	✗
I can	I can't
He/She	He/She ....
They	They ....

2 🔲 A man answers these questions. Listen and write his scores in column A.

Can you cook?

	A	B
Can you make a cup of coffee? (1 point)		
Can you make toast? (1 point)		
Can you cook rice? (3 points)		
Can you make an omelette? (4 points)		
Can you barbecue a chicken? (4 points)		
Can you make a cake? (6 points)		
Can you make your own pasta? (8 points)		
Can you make bread? (10 points)		
Total score		

3 Now find out your partner's scores. Write them in column B.

Sounds: Lovely weather

1 🔲 Listen to these sounds.

/v/ It's never very cold in November.

/w/ What's the weather like in winter?

Listen to the two sounds together.

- I want to watch TV this evening.

It's twenty past twelve.

2 🔲 Listen and practise.

seven have very	wet windy winter
lovely vegetables	Wednesday watch
November TV	sandwich weather

3 Write a sentence. Use words from both boxes.

4 Read out your sentence.

Phrasebook: Would you like ...?

Match the questions with the pictures. What do you think the replies are?

1

Would you like another drink?

Would you like a lift?

Would you like an ice-cream?

2   3

🔲 Listen and check.

A friend is staying with you. Offer him/her the things in the pictures.

Consolidation

have and have got

1 We can often use *have* or *have got*. In these sentences, they mean the same.

I have a radio, but I don't have a TV. ↔	I've got a radio, but I haven't got a TV.
He has long hair. ↔	He's got long hair.

2 Sometimes you can't use *have got*:

✓ I have breakfast at 8 o'clock.
✗ I've got breakfast at 8 o'clock.

✓ I don't have a shower in the morning.
✗ I haven't got a shower in the morning.

3 Say a few true things about yourself.

I have …

I've got …

I don't have …

I haven't got …

A hundred, a hundred and one …

1 Look at these numbers. Can you fill the gaps?

100 a hundred	101 a hundred and one	137 ....
200 two hundred	205	851
1,000 one thousand	1,011 one thousand and eleven	1,054 ....
1,200 one thousand two hundred	2,500	3,651
100,000 a hundred thousand	200,000	1,000,000 a million

2 Read out these sentences.

a 'Eternal God', a tree in California, is 12,000 years old.

b The MGM Grand Hotel in Las Vegas has 5,005 rooms.

c The railway station at Condor in Bolivia is 4,786 metres above the sea.

d Mount Everest, in the Himalayas, is 8,848 metres high.

e The plane Concorde can carry exactly 100 passengers. It can travel at 2,300 kilometres an hour.

Review

Present simple and continuous

When do you wear shorts?

Are you wearing shorts now?

1 Look at these sentences. Which answer the blue question? Which answer the red question?

I wear shorts in hot weather.

I don't wear shorts.

I'm not wearing shorts.

I'm wearing shorts.

I wear shorts when I play tennis.

I always wear shorts.

What about you? When do you wear shorts? Are you wearing shorts now?

2 Ask and answer questions. Use these ideas.

– smoke   – drink coffee   – speak English
– wear a hat   – wear jeans   – wear glasses

Where's the supermarket?

Look at the map. Where's

1 the supermarket?   4 the chemist?
2 the post office?   5 the kiosk?
3 the bank?   6 the bookshop?

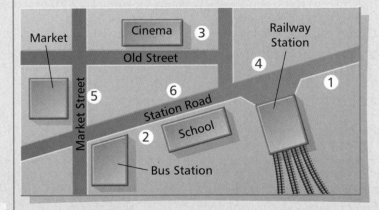

Time

1 Look at the clocks. What time is it?

2 Choose a day of the week. Imagine yourself at these times. Where are you? What are you doing?

---

15 In the past 1

1 Bedtime story

1 Here is a story. The red words are verbs in the *Past tense*.
Read Part 1 of the story and complete the table.

Present	Past
Past simple	

Present	Past
is	was
are	
ask	asked
look	
open	
play	
smile	
want	
give	gave
go	
have	
put	
say	
see	
take	

Part 1

I was about five years old. It was very late at night, and my parents were asleep. I was awake because I wanted to go to the toilet. I went to the toilet, and I saw a light under the living room door. So I opened the door and went in, and I saw a man in the living room. He was about 20 years old.

I looked at him, and he looked at me, and he smiled at me and said, 'Hi! What's your name?' And I said, 'Sam'. 'Do you want to play a game, Sam?' he asked, and I said, 'Yes.' He had a big bag in his hand, and he said, 'OK. Let's put things in this bag.'

So we played the game. I gave things to him, and he put them in his bag. I took my father's wallet out of his jacket, and I took my mother's purse out of her coat, and the man put them in his bag.

Part 2

Then I (1) .... into my parents' bedroom – very quietly – and (2) .... their watches and rings, and my mother's earrings, and (3) .... them to the man.

I (4) .... him some other things too – the silver knives, forks and spoons, two clocks and some old books – and he (5) .... everything in his bag. It (6) .... a great game.

And in the end he (7) .... , 'OK, Sam. It's bedtime. You go back to bed now. Goodnight.' So I (8) .... goodnight and (9) .... back to bed.

2 Read Part 2 of the story. Fill the gaps with verbs from the table.
   Now listen to Sam telling the whole story.

3 Cover the text, and try to tell the story yourself. Use the verbs in the table to help you.

2 Yesterday …

Past simple • time expressions

I saw some old friends on Sunday.

I read nine novels in the summer.

I played football at the weekend.

I went to Istanbul in April.

I wrote a novel in 1989.

I had breakfast at nine o'clock.

I gave my mother some flowers on Wednesday.

I bought a new coat yesterday.

1 Read these sentences. What is the present tense of the red verbs?

2 What can come after *on*, *in* and *at*? Continue these sentences.

I saw her on …

I saw her in …

I saw her at …

3 Write five sentences about yourself (three *true* sentences and two *false* sentences). Use the red verbs.

Read out your sentences. Can other students guess which are true and which are false?

3 Childhood places

(there) was/were • had

… very quiet

… just one room

… a big garden

… one big window

… a small balcony

… lots of trees

… on the third floor

… in the country

… a large veranda

1 Read the notes in the box. Which go with picture A, and which with picture B?

2 Two people remember the places in the pictures. Listen and make the notes into complete sentences.

It was …   There was …

It had …   There were …

What do they say about these things?

Speaker 1 – the rooms   – the sofas
Speaker 2 – the rooms   – the furniture   – the veranda

3 Choose one of these places:

– the place where you lived as a young child
– a place you often visited as a young child

What can you remember about it?

Focus on Form

1 Verb + -ed

play	→	played	smile	→	smiled
stay	→	stayed	like	→	liked
watch	→	....	dance	→	....
wash	→	....	smoke	→	....
listen	→	....	live	→	....

Fill the gaps with a past form from the list.

a When I was a child, we .... in London.

b On Saturday evening, I .... at home and .... television.

c When I was young, I .... the Beatles. I .... to them them all the time.

d He .... 20 cigarettes yesterday.

e I .... my hair this morning.

2 Irregular verbs

Match the present and past forms.

PRESENT
see go put
give write
say buy
have take

PAST
bought said
took went gave
wrote put
saw had

Now test your partner.

What's the past of 'see'?

'Saw'.

3 Time expressions

He went out yesterday.

I saw her at the weekend. 8 o'clock.

We went there in September. the winter. 1975.

I washed my hair on Tuesday.

Fill the gaps with at, on, in or – (= nothing).

a They bought a new car .... Thursday.

b I stayed in bed all day .... yesterday.

c He started the book .... January and finished it .... July.

d I drank a cup of coffee .... 8 o'clock, and I had another cup .... 8.30.

e They went to Australia .... 1998.

4 was & were

Change this description to the past tense.

I lived in an old house in the village of Ashley. It's a very small village – there are [was] about 25 houses, and there's a small shop, [were] too. The school's in the next village. There [was] are 21 children at the school, and there's only one teacher. The teacher is my mother, so we walk there together every morning. [Walked]

When I was a child, I lived in …

How to say it

1   Listen to the *-ed* endings. Practise saying the sentences.

He looked at me.

I smiled at her.

He opened the door.

She asked me a question.

I wanted to go.

2 Listen to the difference between *there are* and *there were*.

There are lots of people at the game.

There were lots of people at the game.

Listen and choose the sentence you hear. Then practise saying it.

There are / There were flowers in the room.

There are / There were two trees near the house.

There are / There were some pictures on the wall.

16 Around the world

1 On the map

1 Look at the six descriptions and find words to add to the lists.

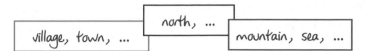

village, town, ...

north, ...

mountain, sea, ...

2 Can you solve the puzzle?

Places to visit

NEWPORT is a large town in the west of the island. It's on the coast.

BELMONTE is a village in the mountains, near the south coast.

IGUANA is the capital of the island. It's a port on the Iguana River, and it's in the east of the island.

JOHNSTOWN is the old capital. It's in the mountains in the centre of the island, and it's on a lake.

SALVADOR is a small town on a river in the north of the island. It's near the coast.

LAGUNA is a small tourist resort on the north coast. It isn't on a river.

What's the best route?

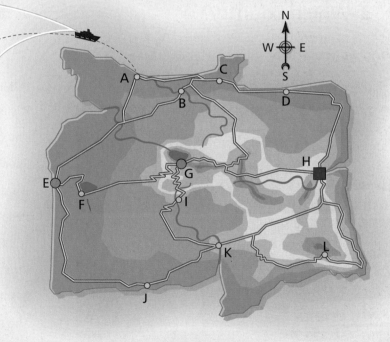

This family of tourists are on a ferry boat, at the start of a week's holiday on the island. They want to go to all six places to visit, and then get the boat home again.

Can you

1 find the six places on the map?

2 tell them the best route?

---

3 Describe some of the other places on the island.

4 Think about your own country. Write about one of these places:

- your home town
- the capital city
- a tourist resort

I come from Limerick. It's a large port in the west of Ireland. It's on the River Shannon.

2 I love you

1 All the gaps in this text are the names of languages. Which language goes in each gap?

Arabic	Greek	Portuguese
Chinese	Italian	Russian
French	Japanese	Spanish
German	Polish	Turkish

2 Here is *I love you* in seven different languages. Can you guess the languages?

Te quiero

Je t'aime

Ich liebe dich

君が好きだよ。

я люблю тебя

Seni seviyorum

أنا أحبك

Can you say *I love you* in any other languages?

The names of languages are often like the countries where people speak them. So (1) .... is the language of Italy, (2) .... is the language of Russia, and (3) .... is the language of Greece. In Turkey people speak (4) .... and in Poland they speak (5) .... In Japan, people speak (6) .... , and in China they speak (7) ....

But some languages are not so simple. People speak (8) .... in many countries in the Middle East and North Africa. People speak (9) .... in Germany, but they also speak it in Austria and part of Switzerland. You can hear (10) .... in France, but also in Canada, Belgium and in many countries in Africa. (11) .... is the language of Portugal, but also of Brazil. And people speak (12) .... not only in Spain, but also in most of South and Central America.

3 Which country?

1 How much do you know about these countries? Match them with the sentences. (Write *I*, *S* or *A*.)

India

Switzerland

Argentina

S	It isn't on the sea.
	It's in Asia.
	The capital is Buenos Aires.
	People speak Spanish there.
	It's a very rich country.
	People speak French, German and Italian there.
	It's a poor country.
	Most of the country is hot in summer and winter.
	It's in Europe.
	The south of the country is very cold.
	The capital is New Delhi.
	It has a lot of lakes and mountains.
	It's in South America.
	The River Ganges flows through it.

2 🔲 Three people say what they know about India, Switzerland and Argentina. Listen and check your answers.

3 Think of a country. Write three or four sentences about it.

Then read out your sentences. Can other students guess the country?

4 International travel

1 These pictures all have a connection with international travel. What do they show?

2 This text is about a business trip.
   Fill the green gaps, using information
   from the pictures.

3 [cassette] You will hear six short scenes.
   Listen and fill the blue gaps.

4 How well did you listen?
   Can you answer these questions?

   a How many bags does Karen check in?
   b Does Karen smoke?
   c How many nights is she staying at the hotel?
   d How many children has she got?
   e What's the weather like in London?

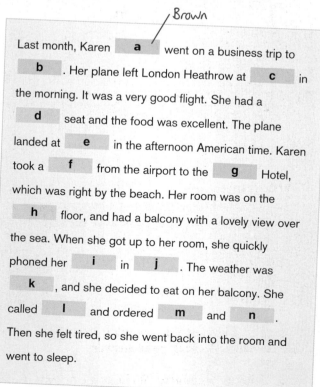

Brown

Last month, Karen [a] went on a business trip to [b] . Her plane left London Heathrow at [c] in the morning. It was a very good flight. She had a [d] seat and the food was excellent. The plane landed at [e] in the afternoon American time. Karen took a [f] from the airport to the [g] Hotel, which was right by the beach. Her room was on the [h] floor, and had a balcony with a lovely view over the sea. When she got up to her room, she quickly phoned her [i] in [j] . The weather was [k] , and she decided to eat on her balcony. She called [l] and ordered [m] and [n] . Then she felt tired, so she went back into the room and went to sleep.

Focus on ... Dates

1 Can you remember these numbers?

1st	2nd	3rd	4th	5th
first	....	third	....	fifth

6th	7th	8th	9th	10th
....	....	eighth	....	....

2 Now try these. What are the missing numbers?

11th	12th	13th	14th	15th
eleventh	twelfth	thirteenth	....	....

16th	17th	18th	19th	20th
....	....	....	....	twentieth

21st	22nd	26th	30th	31st
twenty-first	....	....	thirtieth	....

3 ▭ Six people say the date of their birthday. Write down the dates.

Henry	1st March
André	
Hazel	
Chris	
Natasha	
Gabi	

4 When is your birthday?

Does anyone in the class have the same birthday?

HAPPY BIRTHDAY!

Sounds: Russia, China, Japan

1 ▭ Listen to these sounds.

/ʃ/ She speaks Spanish, Russian and Polish.

/tʃ/ How much chocolate do the children want?

/dʒ/ In June and July we stayed in a small village in Germany.

2 ▭ Listen and practise.

> fish wash shop shirt Russian
> teacher children Chinese watch
> Japan jeans engineer fridge July

3 Write a sentence. Use words from the box.

4 Read out your sentence.

Phrasebook: I'm not sure

What's the capital of India?

1 ▭ Four people answer this question. What do they say?

– .... Bombay.

– .... Calcutta?

– ....

– .... Delhi.

Which answer is correct?

2 Can you answer these questions? Use the expressions in the box.

I think ...	I don't know.
I'm not sure.	I have no idea.

1 Where is Helsinki?

2 Where is Mount Everest?

3 Where can you see a gondola?

4 Where can you hear Koto music?

5 What is Madagascar? Where is it?

6 What is Potocatapetl? Where is it?

7 What is a kiwi? Where can you find one?

Consolidation

Give me the book!

1 Look at these verbs.

give send bring show write

We can use them like this:

I gave some money to the man.
I gave some money to him.
I gave him some money.

I sent a present to my aunt.
I sent some money to her.
I sent her some money.

Bring the book to me!
Bring me the book!

2 Fill the gaps with phrases from the box.

a I *wro...* a letter, but he
  never answered.

b Can you *g....* some money?
  I need to buy some food.

c It was my girlfriend's birthday,
  so I *Sn....* some flowers.

d Why don't you *sh....* your
  photos? I'd love to see them.

e Waiter, we'd like two coffees, please.
  And can you *b....* some more water?

f The children come home at one o'clock. Can
  you .... something to eat?

sent her
give them
give me
wrote him
bring us
show me

in and on

1 Look at the examples.

in Spain	on the coast
in Europe	on the (west) coast
in the north/south/ east/west	on the sea
	on a lake
in the mountains	on Lake Victoria
in the centre	on a river
	on the River Ganges

2 Fill the gaps with *in* or *on*.

a Manaus is .... the north of Brazil. It's
  .... the Amazon River.

b Geneva is .... the west of Switzerland.
  It's .... Lake Geneva.

c Tokyo is .... the east coast of Japan,
  .... East Asia.

d Ecuador is a small country .... South
  America. The capital, Quito, is .... the
  north of the country, high .... the
  Andes. The second city, Guayaquil, is
  .... the coast.

Review

Which word?

Choose the right words.

a OK – we need *a/some*
  pasta, *a/some* cheese,
  a/some large onion,
  a/some tomatoes and
  a/some bottle of white wine.

b We've got *some/any* soap, but we haven't got
  some/any shampoo. And I'm afraid there isn't
  some/any hot water.

c My children eat a lot of bread, but they don't
  eat *much/many* fruit and they don't eat
  much/many vegetables.

d – How *much/many* computer games have you got?
  – Not *much/many*.

e – How *much/many* money have you got?
  – Not *much/many*.

Describing people

Look at these people and answer the questions.

a What do they
  look like?

b What are they
  wearing?

c How old do you
  think they are?

Words

1 Write sensible endings for these sentences. How
  many endings can you think of for each one?

A You can drink …

B You can play …

C You can listen to …

D You can watch …

E You can read …

2 *Student A*: Read out one of your endings.
  Student B: Which sentence does it go with?

17 In the past 2

1 Did and didn't

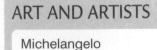

Past simple • positive & negative

1 Do these quiz questions, then check your answers with the teacher. What's your score?

ART AND ARTISTS

Michelangelo

painted
didn't paint

the Mona Lisa.

SCIENCE

The Chinese

made
didn't make

the first fireworks.

FILMS

Steven Spielberg

made
didn't make

the films *Jaws* and *ET*.

HISTORY

Margaret Thatcher

was
wasn't

Britain's first woman Prime Minister.

FAMOUS PEOPLE

Marilyn Monroe

had
didn't have

red hair.

MUSIC

The Beatles

were
weren't

American.

2 Complete these questions, using verbs from the box. What are the answers?

die	died
play	played
start	started
win	won
write	wrote

SPORT

England

the 1998 football World Cup.

FAMOUS PEOPLE

Frank Sinatra

in a plane crash.

MUSIC

Jimi Hendrix

the guitar.

HISTORY

The First World War

in 1914.

BOOKS AND PLAYS

Charles Dickens

the play *Hamlet*.

3 Work with a partner. Choose one of the topics and write a question of your own.

Can other students answer it?

2 Did you see …?

Yes/no questions

1 *Did you See* that programme about hospitals last night?

Yes, I did.

Did you like it ?

Yes, I did. It was quite interesting.

2 *Did watch* the football match on Sunday?

No, I didn't.
Was it good?

Yes, it was.
We won 2–0.

3 *Did you go* the concert yesterday?

No. Did you?

Yes, I did.

Did you enjoy it

No, it was really boring.

enjoy it

1  Listen to the three conversations and fill the gaps.

Practise the conversations.

2 Think of something you saw recently. Ask other students about it.

3 Memory test

Wh- questions

Can you remember …

1 *… your first day at school?*
● What did you wear?
● What was your teacher's name?

2 *… the last time you bought some clothes?*
● What did you buy?
● Where did you buy it?
● How much did it cost?

3 *… last Sunday?*
● What was the weather like?
● What did you eat and drink for breakfast?
● What time did you get up?

4 *… the last time you went to a party?*
● … wear?
● … arrive?
● … leave?

5 *… the last time you ate in a restaurant?*
● Where …?
● What …?
● How much …?

SCORE UP TO 6 POINTS FOR EACH SECTION. TOTAL: 30 POINTS

1 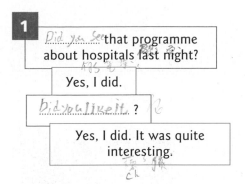 Two people do Part 1 of this memory test. Listen and give each person a score out of 6.

2 Read the whole test. What are the questions for Parts 4 and 5?

3 Here are some verbs from the test. What are their past forms?

    wear   buy   cost   eat   drink   get up   arrive   leave

4 Do the test with a partner. Give your partner a score out of 30.

Focus on Form

1 Irregular verbs

Match the present and past forms.

Present
get make wear
buy cost leave
drink win eat

Past
left cost won
wore made bought
ate got drank

Now test your partner.

What's the past of 'get'?

'Got'.

2 I went ↔ I didn't go

Fill the gaps in this table.

Yesterday I ...

watched TV ↔ didn't watch TV

went to the cinema ↔ didn't go to the cinema

bought a newspaper ↔ .... a newspaper

got up early ↔ .... up early

played cards ↔ .... cards

made a cake ↔ .... a cake

had a big lunch ↔ .... a big lunch

wore a white shirt ↔ .... a white shirt

Which sentences are true of you?

3 Questions in the past

Choose question words from the box, and make *Wh-* questions.

Example:

Did you eat *at home/in the park/in a restaurant?*

→ Where did you eat?

a Did you see *Peter/Mary/John?*

b Did they drink *water/milk/wine?*

c Did she go *home/to the cinema/ to a party?*

d Did they win *£100/£1,000/ £1,000,000?*

e Did he leave *on Tuesday/at the weekend/yesterday?*

What
Who
When
Where
How much

4 was(n't) & were(n't)

Change these sentences to the past.

a He's at school.   →   He was at school.

b They're asleep.   →   ....

c I'm not in Class 1. →   I wasn't in Class 1.

d She isn't at home. →   ....

e We aren't married. →   ....

f Is she at work?   →   ....

g Where is she?   →   ....

h Are you there?   →   ....

i Where are you?   →   ....

Note: didn't = did not   wasn't = was not   weren't = were not

How to say it

1 🔊 Listen to *didn't* and *wasn't* in these sentences. Practise saying them.

I didn't see you at the party.

We didn't go to London.

He wasn't there last night.

The film wasn't very interesting.

2 🔊 Listen to the rhythm of these sentences. Practise saying them.

■ . . ■
What did you wear?

■ . . ■ .
Where did you buy it?

■ . . ■ .
Why did you go there?

■ . ■ . . ■
How much did it cost?

18 How to get there

1 From A to B

1 Where does the person go? Use words from the box.

up	into	over	through
down	out of	across	along

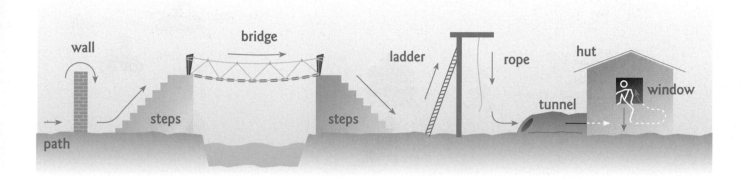

2 Look at this picture. How does the prisoner escape?

He goes …   He climbs …

3 Now listen. Is your answer the same?

2 Getting to work

1 Three people say how they get to work in the mornings.
   Change the pictures into words. Use the expressions in the box.

go by train	drive
go by bus	cycle
go by taxi	walk
station	leave home
bus stop	get to work

A I usually [bus picture]. There's a [bus stop sign] just outside my
   house. If I'm late I sometimes [taxi picture], but it's quite expensive.

B I [train picture]. I always [walk picture] to the [station picture], as it's
   only five minutes from my house. I always [house picture] at 7.30.

C I usually [car picture], but if it's a nice
   day I sometimes [cycle picture].
   I [computer picture] at 8.30.

2 How do you get to work or school in the mornings? What about other people in your family?

3 It's on the left

1 Look at these directions. Can you put them in the right order?

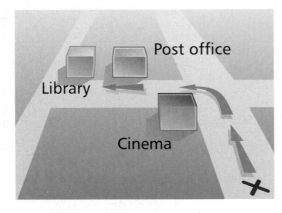

Post office
Library
Cinema

a ☐ The library is at the end of the street, on the right.

b ☐ Then carry straight on.

c ☐ There's a cinema on the corner.

d ☐ Go past the post office.

e 1 Go straight along this road.

f ☐ Turn left at the cinema.

2 [cassette icon] You will hear two people giving directions. Listen and answer the questions.

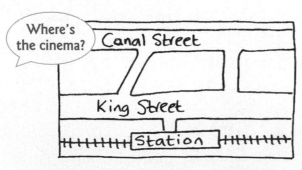

Where's the cinema? Canal Street, King Street, Station

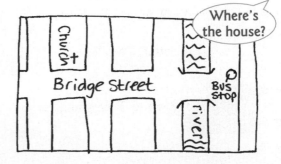

Where's the house? Church, Bridge Street, Bus stop, river

3 Choose one of the maps. Can you give the same directions?

4 Imagine you're meeting a friend somewhere (e.g. at your house, at a restaurant).
   Draw a simple map, and tell your friend how to get there.

4 The island of Odysseus

1 Read the article about the Greek island of Ithaki. Find answers to these questions.

> Are there many tourists?

> What are the beaches like?

> Are there many places to eat?

> What can you do at night?

> Are the roads good?

> Can you camp?

> What can you do during the day?

Islands in the Sun

Ithaki *the island of Odysseus*

Statue of Odysseus, Stavros

Ithaki is a small island – just 30 kilometres long. It's very mountainous, but has good roads. Most of the year, it's very quiet, but in August the tourists arrive, and the harbour in the main town, Vathi, is full of boats. If you want a quiet holiday with warm sunny weather, go in May, June or July.

Frikes • Kioni
Stavros •
• Kathara
Vathi •

Accommodation

Most people stay in rooms, but in August this can be expensive. There are several beaches with cheap camp-sites.

Beaches

The beaches are stony, not sandy. You can drive to some of them, but you need a boat to get to the best beaches on the island.

Eating out

Restaurants are cheap. A few stay open all year round, but in the summer there are lots of places to eat all over the island.

Other places to visit

Drive up the mountain to Kathara Monastery. On a good day, there is a beautiful view of Vathi. Then have coffee in Stavros, see the statue of Odysseus there and visit the museum. And then go on to Frikes or Kioni for a walk by the sea and a meal.

Nightlife

In August there is a music festival, and there are also a few discos and bars with music. In the evenings the main road in Vathi is closed, and children play football and ride their bikes while their parents sit in cafés. In the summer, most places stay open until one or two o'clock.

Vathi

A beach in Ithaki

Kioni

---

2 🎧 Someone describes three ways of getting to Ithaki. Listen and fill the gaps.

From Athens
You .... down to Patras. Then you ....
to Ithaki.

From Kefalonia
You .... across the island. Then you ....
to Ithaki.

From Italy
You .... from Italy to Greece. You .... at Igoumenitsa, and .... down the coast, and then you .... to Ithaki.

Listen again. How long is each journey?

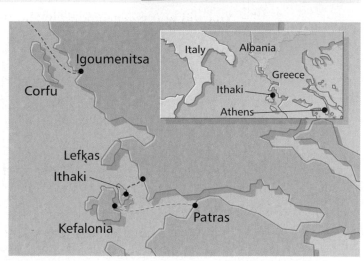

I Study pages

Focus on ... Short answers

1 Look at these questions and answers.

Does she smoke?	Yes, she does. No, she doesn't.
Are they having lunch?	Yes, they are. No, they aren't.
Did he give you the money?	Yes, he did. No, he didn't.

2 Here are some more questions and answers. What are the missing answers?

a Do your children like pizza?   Yes, they do.
 No, ...

b Did you enjoy the party?   Yes, ...
 No, I didn't.

c Are you married?   Yes, ...
 No, I'm not.

d Can he speak German?   Yes, he can.
 No, ...

e Is there any coffee?   Yes, ...
 No, there isn't.

3 Give true answers to these questions.

> Did you come here by bus?

> Are you wearing black shoes?

> Is there a TV in the class?

> Do you have a bike?

> Can you play chess?

> Does your teacher smoke?

> Do you like James Bond films?

Sounds: July and April

1 🔊 Listen to the 'l' sound in English.

He climbed down the ladder.

She left on the eleventh of July.

We stayed in a small hotel.

2 🔊 Listen and practise.

> like flowers play yellow
> England usually salad
> girl small April vegetables
> children beautiful school

3 Write a sentence. Use words from box.

4 Read out your sentence.

Phrasebook: Let's ...

Match the expressions with the pictures.

> Let's ask for the bill.

> Shall we take a taxi?

> Let's get some petrol.

> Shall we dance?

🔊 Listen. What does the other person say?

Imagine it's the end of the lesson.
What do you want to do? Suggest things
to another student.

Consolidation

It isn't very …

1 Choose expressions to describe these dogs.

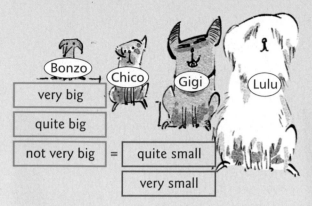

very big

quite big

not very big = quite small

very small

2 Write in the missing adjectives.

a Our flat isn't very big = It's quite small

b Our TV isn't very .... = It's quite cheap

c Our car isn't very .... = It's quite slow

d Their car isn't very old = It's quite ....

e My brother isn't very old = He's quite ....

f My sister isn't very .... = She's quite short

g Her hair isn't very .... = It's quite short

h We aren't very .... = We're quite poor

3 Now talk about one of these:

– your town/village   – your mother/father
– your flat/house   – your brother/sister
– your car/bike   – your boyfriend/girlfriend
– your TV/watch   – your husband/wife

Years

1 Look at the examples. Can you fill the gaps?

1900 nineteen hundred
1901 nineteen hundred and one
1906 ....
1910 nineteen (hundred and) ten
1911 nineteen eleven
1948 nineteen forty-eight
1960 ....
1993 ....
2000 two thousand
2001 two thousand and one
2007 ....

2 Make true sentences. Read out your answers.

The first Mickey Mouse cartoon was		1492.
Steven Spielberg made the film *Jaws*		1903.
Columbus went to America	in	1928.
Henry Ford made his first car		1962.
Marilyn Monroe died		1975.

Review

Climate and weather

Imagine you're in these places.

New York in April   London in December   Moscow in September

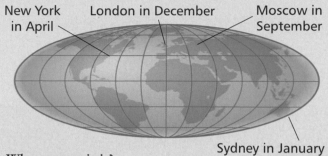

Sydney in January

What season is it?
What do you think the weather's like?

Countries

Which words go with which countries?
Make two or three sentences about each one.

Warsaw   Ottawa
                                    Riyadh

very dry   **CANADA**

                French   The Middle East

Polish   **SAUDI ARABIA**
                                    very large

cold in winter   North America
                                    Arabic

Europe   **POLAND**
                                    English

Do you know anything else about these countries?

Mixed-up words

1 Look at these mixed-up words. Can you make

B E E N M O R V   A E R T W

A C H M R   A B C D O P R U

A C E P R T   C E I J U

– three things to drink?
– three months?
– three things in a room?

How do you spell them?

A B E F R R U Y

A F O S

A D E E L M N O

2 Now you write a mixed-up word. Show it to your partner.

Y O U C D L
(The weather)

19 You mustn't do that!

1 You must stay in your car

must & mustn't • can

1 Read the text about the Kruger National Park.

  a Where is the Kruger National Park?
  b Why do people go there?
  c Where can you stay in the Park?

THE KRUGER NATIONAL PARK covers 20,000 square kilometres. It is the largest wildlife park in South Africa, and a wonderful place to see animals in their natural home. You can drive through the park in your own car, and look at lions, zebras, giraffes, elephants and crocodiles – and you can sometimes see a leopard or a rhinoceros. You can visit the park just for a day, or you can stay overnight at one of the many Rest Camps.

2 Look at the six sentences. Which do you think are true? And which are false?

a You must stay in your car.
b You must take a gun with you.
c You mustn't stop the car.
d You mustn't feed the animals.
e You can take photos.
f You can bring pets into the park.

3 Here is some more information about the Park. Fill the gaps with *can*, *must* or *mustn't*.

1 The Park is very large, so all visitors .... carry a road map. You .... buy a map at the entrance gate.

2 You .... keep to 50 km/h on the main roads, and 40 km/h on the small roads. You .... leave the roads.

3 Day visitors .... leave the Park before 6.00. If you want to stay overnight at a Rest Camp, you .... reserve a room.

4 You .... drive in the Park at night, but if you are staying in a Rest Camp, you .... go on a group tour to see the animals at night.

4 Think about your English class. What are the rules?
Write sentences saying what you *can*, *must* and *mustn't* do.

2 Can I ...?

can • questions with 'can'

1 [cassette] You will hear four short conversations.
What can the woman do? What can't she do?

a She can/can't use the phone.

b She can/can't smoke in the flat.

c She can/can't listen to the news.

d She can/can't have a glass of beer.

2 [cassette] Listen again. What were the questions?
What were the answers?

3 Work in pairs. Turn to page 109. Ask and
answer questions.

3 All in a day's work

have to • don't have to

1 Look at these sentences. What does *I have to* ... mean? What does *I don't have to* ... mean?

a ☐ I have to get up very early.

b ☐ I don't have to get up very early.

c ☐ I have to be polite.

d ☐ You have to be very careful when the weather's bad.

e ☐ I have to be nice to everyone and smile a lot.

f ☐ I have to be away from home a lot.

g ☐ I don't have to work long hours.

h ☐ I don't have to work all year.

i ☐ I have to work late in the evening.

I work as a cleaner in a big hotel. It's not a very nice job ...

2 Three people talk about their jobs.
What do you think they say?
Match the sentences with the people.

I work in an Italian restaurant – I'm a waitress. It's quite a nice job ...

I work on a fishing boat. It's a hard job and it's quite dangerous ...

[cassette] Now listen and check your answers.

3 Think about what you do. What are the good things
about it? What are the bad things? Tell your partner.

I have to ...

I don't have to ...

Focus on Form

1 must & mustn't

You must	=	Do it!
You mustn't	=	Don't do it!

What do these signs mean?
Make sentences from the table.

You must You mustn't	wear a hard hat. stop. smoke. drive slowly. turn left. park your car. turn your lights on.

2 can & can't

> In Britain, you can often buy food at petrol stations (but you can't buy petrol at the supermarket).

Think about your own country. Are these sentences true or false?

a You can buy food at petrol stations.
b You can smoke on buses and trains.
c You can buy alcohol on Sundays.
d You can smoke in restaurants.
e You can carry a gun.
f Children can buy cigarettes and alcohol.
g You can buy petrol at the supermarket.

3 have to & don't have to

I have to go.	They don't have to go.
She has to go.	He doesn't have to go.

Fill the gaps with *have to*, *has to*, *don't have to* or *doesn't have to*.

a I love Sundays because I .... get up and go to work. My husband's a taxi driver, so he often .... work at the weekend.
b Sorry, I can't come out tonight – I .... clean the flat.
c My son's seven years old. He .... go to school, but he .... do any homework.
d You can stay here – you .... go.

How to say it

1 🔲 **Listen to *must* and *mustn't* in these sentences. Practise saying them.**

You must take a coat.

You must tell me about it.

You mustn't take photos.

You mustn't feed the animals.

You mustn't say anything.

2 🔲 **Listen to the sound of *can* and *can't*. Practise saying the sentences.**

You can come with us if you like.

– Can I come?
– Of course you can.

Sorry, you can't come with us.

– Can I watch the news?
– No, sorry, you can't.

20 The body

1 Aliens

1 Imagine you're a human space traveller in this bar. Which aliens are friendly? Which are unfriendly?

2 Find words in the text to label the diagram.

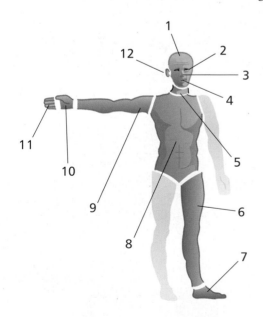

3 Choose one of the unfriendly aliens in the bar. How could you describe it?

Friendly aliens

Before you talk to an alien, be sure that it's friendly. Be very careful – there are millions of different types of alien, and it's easy to make a mistake.

These aliens are friendly to humans:

🛸 **Gnergs** are yellow or green. They have three long thin legs, three arms, and three fingers on each hand. They have one eye in the middle of their head, and a long thin nose.

🛸 **Zaps** can be any colour. They have a long thin body and eight legs. They have two heads. Each head has a large mouth and two eyes on long stalks.

🛸 **Bolonids** look a bit like humans, but they have a small body and small arms and legs. They are light green, and have large black eyes and no ears.

🛸 **Bzerks** have one long leg, two arms and no head. They have one big eye at the top of their body. They are usually red or purple.

🛸 **Ogons** also look a bit like people, but they have a small head on the end of a very long neck. They are green with short legs and large white hands and feet.

2 Are you an athlete?

1 Match the verbs with the pictures.

2 🔊 A woman does this quiz. Listen and give her a score out of 50.

catch	run
climb	stand
jump	swim
kick	throw
ride	walk

A B C D E
F G H I J

Can you ...

1 ... **run 100 metres?** (1 point)
... **run 5 kilometres?** (5 points)

2 ... **swim 100 metres?** (2 points)
... **swim 1 kilometre?** (5 points)

3 ... **ride a bike?** (1 point)
... **ride a bike with no hands?** (3 points)

4 ... **climb up a ladder?** (1 point)
... **climb up a rope?** (6 points)

5 ... **jump over a stream 1 metre wide?** (1 point)
... **jump over a wall 1 metre high?** (4 points)

6 ... **catch a tennis ball in one hand?** (1 point)
... **throw a tennis ball 50 metres?** (3 points)
... **kick a football 100 metres?** (3 points)

7 ... **stand on your head?** (4 points)
... **walk on your hands?** (10 points)

3 Ask your partner the questions. How many points does he/she score?

3 Action!

1 Here are some scenes from a TV advertisement for a chocolate bar. What is the man doing in scenes 2–8? Use these verbs.

climb   drive   fly   jump   ride   run   swim

What's happening in scenes 1 and 9?

2 Look at these past forms. What are the past forms of the other verbs in the box?

climbed   drove

3 Now read the story on page 108.
Tell the story, using verbs in the box instead of *went*.

4 Look at the pictures again. Can you tell the story in your own words?

4 I did it!

1 Look at the pictures. What do you think happens when you do a bungee jump? Put the sentences in the right order.

| | The cage comes down slowly. |

| | You jump. |

| | You get in the cage and they close the door. |

| | They give you a certificate. |

| | You pay. |

| | You take off the harness. |

| | You put on a harness. |

| | You go up in the cage. |

| | They open the door of the cage. |

| | They fix the elastic to the harness. |

2 You will hear someone describing his first bungee jump. Before you listen, look at these questions.

a The speaker uses these adjectives. What is he talking about?

expensive	long	strong
high	big	thick	small

b Where do they fix the two ends of the elastic?

c How high are you when you jump?

d How do you know when you have to jump?

e How do you get down?

🔲 Now listen and answer the questions.

3 Imagine bungee jumping comes to your town. Would you jump?

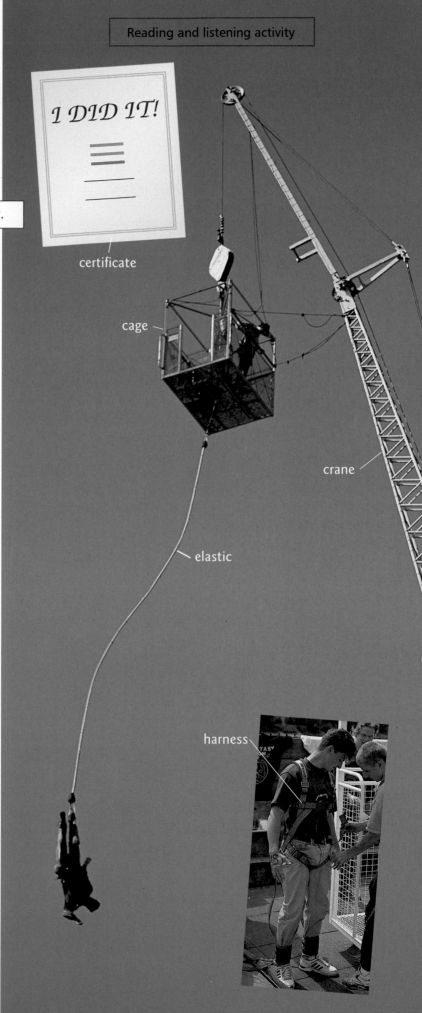

I DID IT!

certificate

cage

crane

elastic

harness

Unit 20 The body   85

J Study pages

Focus on ... Adverbs

Here is part of a story. The green words are all *adverbs*.

I woke suddenly at 6 o'clock. Marie was by my bed. 'Get dressed quickly,' she said, 'or we'll be late.'

When I was ready, we closed the front door quietly and got in the car. Marie drove well – fast but carefully – and we got to the harbour by 7 o'clock. The boat was there, and we jumped in.

As we moved slowly out of the harbour, a black car came round the corner. It was Carlos.

'Marie! Come back!' he shouted angrily. But he was too late.

1 Read the story and complete the table.

2 Complete this rule.

To form an adverb, we usually add .... to the adjective.

Adjective	Adverb
quiet	quietly
slow	
quick	
sudden	
careful	
angry	
fast	
good	

3 Add adverbs to these sentences.

He learns languages.   We drove into town.

I opened the door and went out.

'What do you want?' she asked.

She wrote her name on a piece of paper.

4 Write a true sentence about yourself. Use one of the adverbs in the table.

Sounds: A room in Australia

1 🔲 Listen to the sound 'r' in English.

/r/ I can read Arabic, but I can't write it very well.

Listen to these sounds: /br/, /fr/, /tr/, /dr/, /θr/.

We drove through France.

She worked as a waitress in Australia.

For three days, I had only bread and fruit.

2 🔲 Listen and practise.

room	friend	Britain	country	drive
tourists	France	bring	trousers	bedroom
	wearing	from	bread	dry

3 Write a sentence. Use words from the box.

4 Read out your sentence.

Phrasebook: Could you ...?

This person is ill in bed. He mustn't eat fat, drink alcohol or smoke.

🔲 Listen to the conversation and fill the gaps.

– Could you bring me .... ?
– Yes, of course.
– And could you buy me .... ?
– No, sorry.

Imagine you are the person in bed. Ask for these things.

Consolidation

Verbs with *to, at* and *about*

1 Look at these examples.

to

listen to the radio   go to the cinema   talk to a friend

at

look at someone   arrive at the station   stay at a hotel

about

think about a problem   talk about the weather   read about dinosaurs

2 Fill the gaps with one of the red verbs.

a Why don't you *stay at* my flat? You can sleep on the sofa.

b Shall we *listen to* the news on the radio?

c What time does the plane *arrive at* Heathrow?

d I never *think about* work when I'm at home in the evening.

e I usually *go to* the shops on Saturday.

f I never *look at* her, because she never listens.

Review

Words

Add words to these lists.

a week, minute, day, *Monday Tuesday Wedn*

b cinema, station, library, *bus stop*

c engineer, teacher, shop assistant, *cofe shop*

d car, plane, *train*

e hall, bedroom, *living room*

Verbs in the past

What are the past forms of the verbs in the boxes? Use them to fill the gaps.

a A tall woman *opened* the door. She *was* about 60 years old, and she *had* long grey hair. 'Who are you?' she *asked* me. 'I'm Tom,' I *said*. 'I'm your son.'

be
say
ask
open
have

b Yesterday *was* my sister's birthday, so I *went* to the shops to buy her a present. She *bought* a new jacket, but the jackets _____ very expensive. So I _____ her a pair of jeans.

be
be
buy
want
go

c When we *was* children, we *played* football every day after school, and we *watche* it on TV every weekend.

be
watch
play

Who died when?

How do you say these dates? Make true sentences.

Queen Victoria		30th May 1431.
Abraham Lincoln		23rd April 1616.
Charlie Chaplin	died on	14th April 1865.
Joan of Arc		22nd January 1901.
William Shakespeare		25th December 1977.

21 Good, better, best

1 A better place to live

Comparison of adjectives

1 Look at these sentences. Which are true of your country?

☐ It has a warm climate. ☐ It's a safe place to live. ☐ It's an expensive place to live.

☐ It's a rich country. ☐ The people are friendly. ☐ The roads are dangerous.

☐ The cities are clean. ☐ The food is good. ☐ It's a beautiful country.

Does your partner have the same answers?

2 Choose one other country, and compare it with your own country.
Which do you think

– is warmer?   – is safer?   – is more expensive?

– is richer?   – has friendlier people? – has more dangerous roads?

– is cleaner?   – has better food?   – is more beautiful?

Are there any other differences?

3 Which country do you think is a better place to live? Why?
Write one or two sentences.

> I think .... is a better place to
> live than .... because ...

2 Which is better?

Comparison of adjectives • than

1 A man buys a camera in a shop. Listen to the conversation. Which camera does he buy? Why?

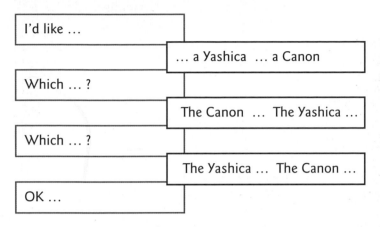

I'd like …

… a Yashica … a Canon

Which … ?

The Canon … The Yashica …

Which … ?

The Yashica … The Canon …

OK …

2 Listen again and complete these notes.

3 Practise the conversation, using the notes.

3 Do you agree?

Superlatives

1 Read the text and find words to complete the table.

high	higher	the highest
big	bigger	biggest
beautiful	more beautiful	most beautiful
good	better	best

2 What are your answers to the questions in the text? Do you all agree or not?

3 Think of a question yourself. You can ask about your town, your country or the world.

Ask other people your question. Do they all agree?

AGREE OR DISAGREE?

It's easy to agree about some things. Everyone agrees, for example, that Mount Everest is the highest mountain in the world, that Russia is the biggest country in the world, and that the Eiffel Tower is the tallest building in Paris.

Other questions are more difficult. For example, what's the most beautiful city in the world? Is it Paris? Rio de Janeiro? Rome? Istanbul? Cape Town? Hong Kong? Prague …?

And what about these questions?
• What's the most beautiful building in your country?
• Who's the most famous person in the world?
• Who's the most dangerous person in the world?
• Who's the best actor in your country?
• What's the best programme on TV?

Ask ten people these questions, and you'll probably get ten different answers.

Focus on Form

1 Adjectives

Write in the missing forms.

cheap	cheaper	the cheapest
tall	taller	
young	younger	
friendly	friendlier	the friendliest
easy	easier	the easiest
happy	happier	
big	bigger	the biggest
hot	hotter	
expensive	more expensive	the most expensive
dangerous	more dangerous	
interesting		
good		the best

2 Comparing

Which of these sentences is true?

Cars are safer than planes.
Cars are more dangerous than planes.

Correct these sentences.

a Mexico is bigger than Brazil. False
b Ronaldo is older than Prince Charles.
c Taxis are cheaper than buses.
d Britain is hotter than California.
e   Chess is easier than noughts and crosses.

3 The biggest mouth

> Koko has the biggest mouth.
> Albie has the shortest hair.

Talk about each of the clowns.

big	small	hair	eyes
long	short	ears	mouth
fair	dark		nose

How to say it

1 🔲 Listen to *than* in these sentences. Practise saying them.

This is better than my old flat.

New York's more interesting than Washington.

He's friendlier than his brother.

Germany's colder than Italy.

2 🔲 Listen to the sounds *-est* and *most*. Practise saying the sentences.

It's the biggest in the world.

It's the best place in the world.

It's the most beautiful building.

Which hotel is the most expensive?

22 Free time

1 Going out

Friends *and* Family *are* No 1!

It's the weekend. There's no work and there's no school. Millions of people all over Britain are spending the day at home. Millions of others are going out. **But where are they going?**

Well, now we know. A new report from Edinburgh University lists the Top 10 things that people do when they go out at the weekend.

The *Top* 10 Activities

1 visit friends or relatives

2 go out for a drink or a meal

3 go for a walk or a bike ride

4 go shopping for fun

5 go to a cinema, concert or sports event

6 do an outdoor sport

7 do an indoor sport

8 follow an interest or hobby

9 go for a drive or a picnic

10 go swimming

1 Read the article, then look at the people. Where do you think they're going?
Choose from *The Top 10 Activities*.

2 [cassette] A man talks about the activities in the list.
What are his top *five* activities?

3 What do you do when you go out? Write a list of your top five activities.

Show your list to another student. Say where you go and what you do.

2 I like spending money

1 Read about person A. What do the other three people like doing?

A

I like doing quiet things. I like reading and painting pictures, and I enjoy walking in the country.

B

I enjoy doing physical exercise. I like 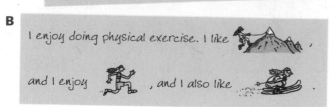,

and I enjoy , and I also like .

C

I like having a good time and spending lots of money. I like  and ,

and I also enjoy . *driving*

D

I like meeting new people. I enjoy ,

and I like . And if I'm on a bus

or train, I really enjoy *talking*

2 Which of the four people would you like to spend the day with? Why?

3 Write down two things you *like* doing, and two things you *don't like* doing.

Does your partner agree?

> I like watching TV in bed.
> I like looking in shop windows.
> I don't like getting up early in the morning.
> I don't like cooking.

3 Sports

1 Work with a partner. Answer the questions together.

sports in your area – how much do you know?

1 What's the name of your local football team? Where do they play?

What other sports can you go and watch?

2 Can you do these sports in your area? If so, where?

tennis   volleyball   golf

3 Where can you go swimming
– indoors?   – out of doors?

4 Where is the *nearest* place to go
skiing?   windsurfing?   climbing?

5 Can you answer these questions?

I need to lose some weight. Are there any exercise classes?

Where's the best place to go running?

2 Discuss the answers together. How well did you do?

3 Role-play

Student A: You are a visitor to the area, and you want to know about sports. Ask B some questions.
Student B: Try to answer A's questions.

4 The curse of the new ground

1 Before you read, find out what a *curse* is.
Then check that you know the meaning of:

– a football ground	– supporters	– a stadium	– win a match
– a football team	– a manager	– an accident	– lose a match

2 Read the story. Can you put Parts 2–8 in the right order?

 **strange stories** There are many strange stories about football, but this is the strangest of them all

The curse of the new ground

1 United were one of the best football teams in the country. They had a lot of supporters, but their ground wasn't very big.

The woman said no, so the police came and moved her. But as she left, she shouted, 'United will never win a match on this land! Remember my words!'

In the end, they finished the stadium, and 40,000 supporters came to watch the first match. United lost the match 5–0.

They started to build the new stadium, but they had lots of problems. One of the walls fell down, and two workers died in strange accidents.

They wanted to move to a bigger ground. So they bought some land on the edge of the city. There was nothing on this land except for one small cottage.

The next year, the same thing happened. The team's manager left, and a new one came – but it made no difference. United lost all their home matches.

An old woman lived in this cottage. 'We're sorry,' the club told her, 'but you have to go. We want to build a new stadium on this land.'

That season, United won lots of matches in other football grounds. But they lost all the matches they played at home.

9 So now, United Football Club want .... But there's one big problem: ....

3 🔲 Now listen to someone telling the story. Were you right? How does the story end?

4 What do you think of the story? Do you agree with any of these statements?

> I think it's true. Things like that happen all the time.

> I don't really believe the story. Maybe United just aren't a very good team.

> I think the whole story is untrue. Things like that are impossible.

K Study pages

Focus on ... Verb + to

1 Look at these examples.

I want an ice-cream.
I want to have a shower.
Do you want to go out?

I'd like a glass of orange juice.
I'd like to watch a video.
Would you like to see my photos?

I need some new shoes.
I need to phone my mother.

I have to get up early in the morning.

2 🔲 Listen to the conversations, and fill the gaps.

1 – .... come to the
cinema this evening?
– No, sorry. ....
come, but ....
do my homework.

2 – .... go and see
a film this evening?
– No, thanks. There's a
football match on, and
.... watch it.

3 – .... go to the
cinema tonight?
– Yes, fine.
– .... go for
a drink first?
– OK. .... wash
my hair. But I can meet
you at about 6.30.

3 Write a sentence about

– something you have to do this week.
– something you need to buy.
– something you want to do this evening.
– something you'd like to do this year.

Sounds: Girls, cars, sport and computers

1 🔲 The letter *r* is often silent, but only in British English. Listen to these sentences in British and American English.

/ɑː/ You can bring your car into the car-park.

/ɔː/ You must do more sport.

/ɜː/ She's a German girl.

/ə/ Put the letters by the computer.

2 🔲 Listen and practise.

car	carpet	cards	market
door	floor	short	fork
girl	dirty	church	worse
exercise	mirror	centre	better

3 Write a sentence. Use words from the box.

4 Read out your sentence.

Phrasebook: What did you say?

🔲 Listen to the conversations. What do the other people say?

Listen to the teacher. Tell him/her if you don't understand!

Focus on ... Verb + to

Consolidation

go

1 Look at these examples.

go to { a concert / the shops

go to { school / bed

go { out / home

go { swimming / shopping

go for { a walk / a drink

2 **What about these? Add *to*, *in* or – (= nothing).**

a go .... work   f go .... a football match
b go .... a meal   g go .... the cinema
c go .... running   h go .... the toilet
d go .... church   i go .... a picnic
e go .... a drive   j go .... a party

3 **Think about last week. What did you do? Make sentences.**

I went ...   *I didn't go ...*

Review

Where is it?

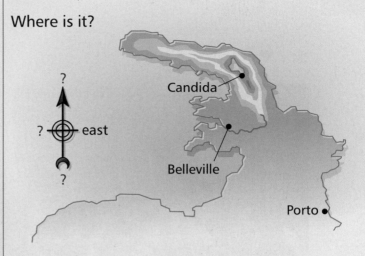

What are the missing directions?

Where are Porto, Belleville and Candida?

Positive and negative

Finish these sentences using a negative form.

> Chips are very nice, but ...
> ... they aren't very healthy.

a He's very rich, but ...
b There's a radio in my room, but ...
c There were lots of men at the party, but ...
d We've got some bread, but ...
e The hotel has got a restaurant, but ...
f I can play the guitar, but ...

Now finish these sentences.

g I like chocolate, but ...
h She smokes, but ...
i I have to wear a jacket at work, but ...
j They gave me a birthday card, but ...

Time words

Here are some sentences from earlier pages. Fill the gaps with *at*, *in* or *on*.

a .... the summer, Istanbul is quite hot.
b We go to church .... Sunday.
c It starts .... ten past eight, and finishes .... nine o'clock.
d Spring comes late in Moscow, usually .... April or May.
e I don't have a shower .... the morning.
f I played football .... the weekend.
g I bought a new coat .... October.
h What do you do .... New Year's Eve?
i I wrote a novel .... 1989.

1 I ♥ Paris

(I'm) going to

1 Read about the people at the airport. When do we use *going to*?

These people are just arriving at Charles de Gaulle Airport. They're going to spend a few days in Paris.

Joanna is going to stay with her uncle, who works for Air France.

Alfonso is in Paris on business, but he's going to have some free time in the evenings.

Mike and Lisa are going to spend two or three days in Paris and then they're going to drive down to the south of France.

2 They say what they're going to do in Paris. Listen and complete the sentences.

 Joanna is going to buy …
She's going to visit …
In the evening, she's going to …

Alfonso is going to stay …
He's going to visit …
In the evening, he's going to …

Mike and Lisa are going to stay …
They're going to sit …
They're going to drink …
In the evening, they're going to …

Imagine you can go to Paris too. Who would you like to go with?

3 Choose a place to visit, and write down three things you're going to do.

   Read out your sentences.
   Can other students guess the place?

I'm going to climb Mount Fuji.
I'm going to eat sushi.
I'm going to

2 Do you plan ahead?

1 Ask you partner questions about next weekend.

   If your partner is *sure* of the answer, write
   ✓ (= *Yes*) or ✗ (= *No*) beside the question.

   If your partner *isn't sure*, write **?** .

Are you going to get up late?

Yes, I am.   No, I'm not.   I'm not sure.

✓ Too   ✗ 张雪明   ?

2 Count the number of times you wrote **?**.

   Mark your partner's place on this scale.

You plan things carefully and know exactly what you're going to do.	0	1	2	3	4	5	6	7	8	9	10	You don't like planning. You just wait and see what happens.

3 Think of a question of your own. Ask other students your question.

   How many say *Yes*? How many say *No*? How many aren't sure?

Questions with 'going to'

Next weekend, are you going to ...

✗	... get up late?
✗	... do any housework?
✓	... go out for a meal?
✓	... write to anyone?
✗	... visit anyone?
✗	... do any sport?
✓	... go for a walk?
✓	... watch TV?
✓	... read a book?
✗	... buy any clothes?

---

3 Help!

Present continuous

1 [cassette] You will hear two short conversations. Listen and answer the questions.

   a What is Paul doing at the weekend?
   b What does he ask?
   c What are the other people doing? Complete the table.

	Saturday	*Sunday*
1	She's ...	
2	He's ...	

2 Imagine that Paul wants your help. What do you say?

3 Imagine you want to do one of these things this weekend.

paint your kitchen

move a piano

clean your flat

look after four small children

Try to find someone to help you!

Focus on Form

| Mike | Sheila | Carole | George | Anna |

1 going to

> am / is / are + going to + verb

These five people are coming back from the shops. Look at their shopping, and match the bubbles with the people.

a I'm going to paint the kitchen.

b I'm going to have a pizza.

c I'm going to take some photos.

d I'm going to wash some clothes.

e I'm going to play a computer game.

What other things are they going to do?

Mike's going to watch a video.

Sheila's going to ...

2 Are you going to ... ?

Student A: Imagine you are one of the people.
Student B: Ask questions. Who is A?

Are you going to read a book?

No, I'm not Anna.

Are you going to ...

3 Present continuous

These sentences are about the future.

This evening, I'm having a driving lesson.
On Friday, some friends are coming to stay.
On 15th June, my brother's getting married.
In the summer, we're all going to France.

What about you? Write sentences about yourself and your family.

How to say it

1 📼 Listen to *going to* in these sentences. Practise saying the sentences.

I'm going to clean my room.

He's going to buy a new suit.

We're going to visit some friends.

She's going to stay with her uncle.

2 📼 Listen to the rhythm of these sentences. Practise saying them.

. .. . ■ .. . ■
I'm going to buy her a present.

. . .. . ■ . . ■
Are you going to change some money?

. . .. . ■ . .
Is she going to write to us?

. . .. . . ■ .
Are they going to stay at our house?

---

24 Feelings

1 I'm hungry!

1 Look at these people. How do they feel? Use words from the box.

hungry	hot	tired
thirsty	cold	ill

2 Look at the pictures in the bubbles. What do you think the people are saying?

Why don't you … ?   Shall I … ?   Let's …

Now listen. Did the people say the same as you?

3 How do you feel at the moment? Do you feel hungry? thirsty? hot? …? Tell your partner.

2 I felt really …

1 Here are some sentences from stories. Can you find six other words which describe people's feelings? Write them in the table.

excited
....
....
....
....
....
....

'We're meeting the President tomorrow,' he said. 'Aren't you excited?' 'No, not really,' I replied.

'There's a letter for you,' she said. I opened it. I was surprised to see it was from my brother in California.

'What's wrong with Alice?' I asked. 'Oh, nothing. She's upset because her best friend didn't invite her to his birthday party. That's all.'

He didn't know if he was happy or sad. He wanted to laugh and cry at the same time.

Her face was white. She stood there, and said nothing, but I could see that she was angry.

He held the knife a few centimetres from my face. 'I mustn't show that I'm frightened,' I told myself.

2 Imagine that these things happen. How would you feel?

   a You win a holiday for two in Paris.
   b Someone writes you a letter which begins 'You don't know me, but actually I'm your sister …'
   c You're in bed when someone throws a large stone through your bedroom window.
   d Your favourite film star dies.

3 Talk about something that happened to you. Include the sentence in the bubble.

I felt really ....!

3 Did you enjoy it?

1 🎞 You will hear four people talking about these videos. Two of them watched *Titanic* and two of them watched a *Mr Bean* video.

Listen and complete the table.

	Which video did they watch?	Did they enjoy it?	What do they say about it?
Speaker 1			
Speaker 2			
Speaker 3			
Speaker 4			

2 Choose a video, film or TV programme that you saw recently. Write down what you thought of it.

3 Find other students who saw the same thing. Do they agree with you?

I didn't enjoy THE ENGLISH PATIENT. It was very long and boring, and it was also very sad.

HOME ALONE is a children's film, but it was very funny and I laughed a lot. I enjoyed it.

4 Showing your feelings

1 Try this experiment.

- Look at these photos. Which of the people do you think are

  – happy?
  – sad?
  – angry?
  – surprised?
  – frightened?

  Compare your answers with other students. Are they the same?

- Do people show feelings in the same way in all the countries of the world? Do we all smile when we're happy, and cry when we're sad?

  What do you think?

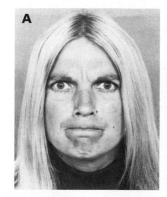
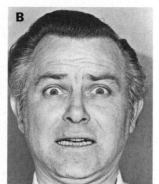
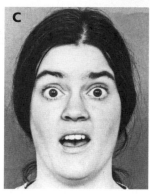

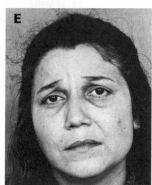

© Paul Ekman, 1975

2 Now read about Paul Ekman. Can you fill the gaps in the story?

Paul Ekman is an American scientist. He wanted to know the answer to this question: Do people show feelings in the same way everywhere in the world?

Ekman took photos of (1) .... Some people looked happy, some looked sad, some looked angry, some looked surprised, and some looked frightened. He showed the photos to (2) .... , and asked them to match the feelings with the faces. He found that everyone could do this quite easily: everyone agreed which people were happy, which were sad, which were angry, and so on.

Then Ekman went to (3) .... In this village, people had no television, they saw no films, and they never saw people from other countries. So they didn't know what people from other countries looked like. Ekman showed his photos to (4) .... , and asked them the same questions : Which people are happy? Which are sad? Which are angry? He found that even here they could answer the questions quite easily.

So Ekman's conclusion was:

the people in this village

people from 21 countries

people in the USA

a village in Papua New Guinea

What do you think Ekman's conclusion was?

3 🔲 **Someone describes Paul Ekman's experiment. Listen and fill the gaps in the story.**

Final review

Imagine

Choose a month, and imagine a scene with you in it.

Use these questions to help you.

Where are you? What are you wearing? What are you doing?

What season is it? What time of day is it? What's the weather like?

Are there any other people? What are they doing?

Yesterday

Which of these things do you think your partner

– did yesterday?
– didn't do yesterday?

Write ten sentences.

 eat rice

 ride a bike

 go shopping

 climb up a ladder

 swim

 make a cup of coffee

 drive a car

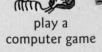 play a computer game

 buy a drink

 write a letter

Now ask questions and find out.
How many did you get right?

Interview

Student A: You work for a radio station in your town. You are going to interview a tourist. Here are your notes. What questions are you going to ask?

- Name
- From ... (town, country)
- ... years old
- Married? Children? How many?
- Job
- Arrived ...
  Is leaving ...

- Is staying at ...
- Is/isn't having a good time
- Likes/doesn't like
  – the town
  – the people
  – the food
- Is/isn't going to come again

Student B: You are a tourist. A is going to interview you. What are you going to say?

Now have the interview.

Can you remember?

All of these pictures are from earlier units. Choose one of the pictures.
What can you remember about it?

A EMPIRE STATE

B

C

D

E

F

G

H

I

J
Frikes
Kioni
Stavros
Kathara
Vathi

K

L

Additional material

1.2 Photos

Student A

1 one

my room – very small

2 two

my bike – new

3 three

my friend – from London

4 four

?

Student B

1 one

my house – very big

2 two

my car – a Porsche

3 three

my friend – a film star

4 four

?

3.3 What's this?

Student A: Ask questions with *Who*, *What* and *Where*.
Student B: Answer the questions. (If you don't know the answer, look in the box!)

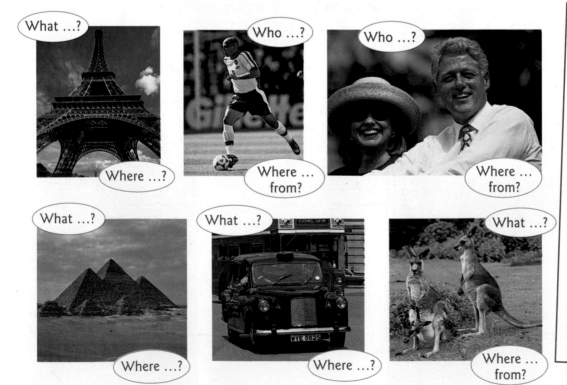

What ...?
Who ...?
Who ...?
Where ...?
Where ... from?
Where ... from?
What ...?
What ...?
What ...?
Where ...?
Where ...?
Where ... from?

In London, the taxis are black and the buses are red.

Kangaroos are from Australia.

Ronaldo is a footballer. He's from Brazil.

The Eiffel Tower is in Paris. It's 300 metres high.

Bill and Hillary Clinton are from the USA.

The Pyramids are near Cairo, in Egypt. They're 4,500 years old.

2.2 How old are they?

André

Olga

Greg

Kumiko

Caterina

4.1 Painting by numbers

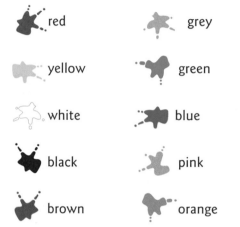

red

grey

yellow

green

white

blue

black

pink

brown

orange

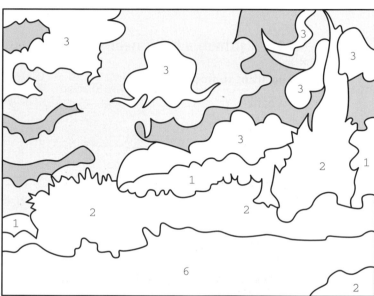

Vincent Van Gogh: Wheatfield with Cypresses

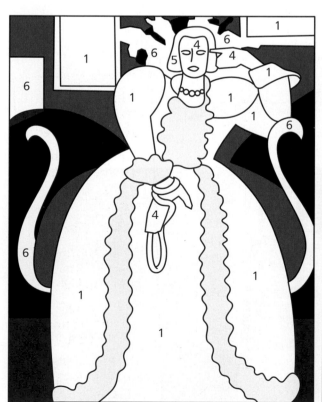

Henri Matisse: Lady in Blue

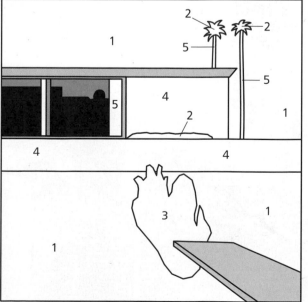

David Hockney: A bigger splash

4.3 **Where's my ...?** *Student A*

You can't find

– your shoes
– your ball
– your glasses

Ask Student B.

Now answer
B's questions.

10.3 Is there a bank near here? *Student A*

You want to find

– a bank
– a post office
– a bookshop

Ask Student B.

Now answer
B's questions.

① = a chemist
② = a newsagent
③ = a restaurant

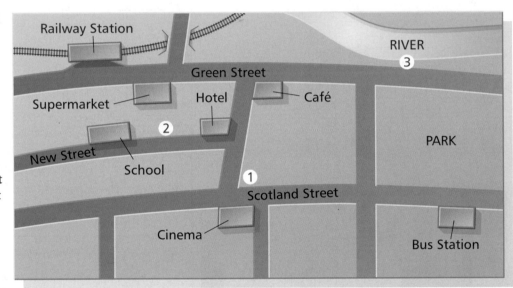

12.3 Who do you mean?

5.3 Buildings

In the Empire State Building …

… there are 102 floors.

… there are nearly 2,000 stairs between the ground floor and the top floor.

… there are 7–12 rooms on each floor.

… there are 73 lifts.

… there are five restaurants.

… there are about ten shops.

… there isn't a swimming pool.

5 Focus on Form Yes/no questions

9.2 What do you do?

Choose a role for yourself, and write it on a piece of paper.

I'm	a student. I study	music		Cambridge.		Church Street.
	a teacher. I teach	business	at a college in	Edinburgh.	I live in	King Street.
		English		Manchester.		Market Street.

4.3 Where's my ...? *Student B*

Answer Student A's questions.

Now ask A. You can't find

– your umbrella
– your pens
– your camera

10.3 Is there a bank near here? *Student B*

Answer Student A's questions.

① = a bank
② = a post office
③ = a bookshop

Now ask A. You want to find

– a chemist
– a newsagent
– a restaurant

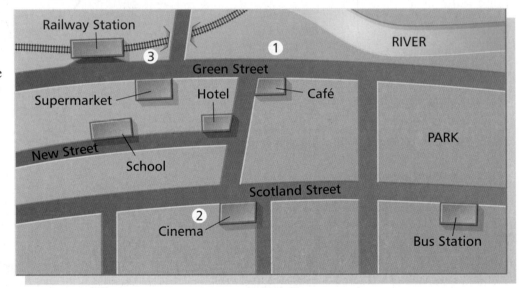

20.3 Action!

I remember I once saw an advertisement on TV for a chocolate bar. It showed a very good-looking man at home with his very beautiful wife. His wife asked him to get her a chocolate bar, so he said 'Just a moment, darling', got up and quickly put on his running shoes. Then he *went* out of the house, got into his car, and *went* to a small airport. There he got into a helicopter and *went* across the sea to an island. On the beach there was a white horse. He got on the horse, and *went* across the island until he came to a bridge over a big river. In the middle of the river there was a very high rock. He *went* off the bridge into the river, and *went* to the rock. Then he *went* up the rock, and right at the top there was a chocolate bar, in gold paper. He took the chocolate bar, and brought it back to his wife. What I never understood was – why didn't he just go round to his local supermarket and buy one?

19.2 Can I …? *Student A*

1 You are a guest in B's flat. You want to

- have a shower
- phone your mother
- have a sleep
- have a banana
- play a computer game

Ask questions with *Can I …?*

2 This is your flat. B is your guest. Answer his/her questions.

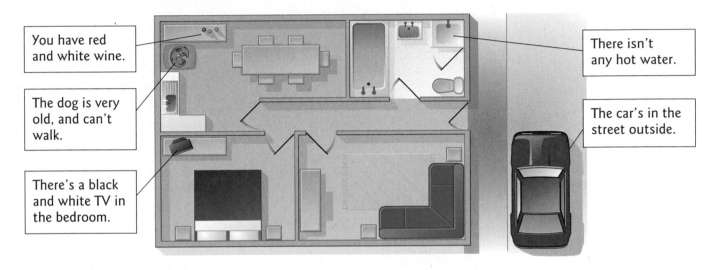

You have red and white wine.

The dog is very old, and can't walk.

There's a black and white TV in the bedroom.

There isn't any hot water.

The car's in the street outside.

19.2 Can I …? *Student B*

1 This is your flat. A is your guest. Answer his/her questions.

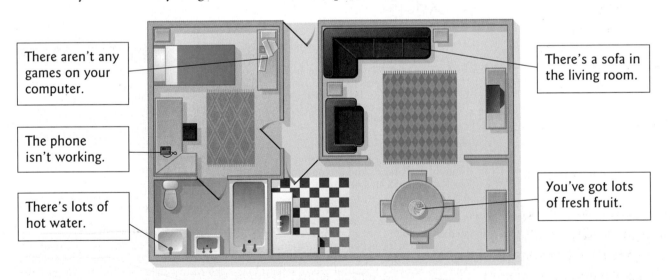

There aren't any games on your computer.

The phone isn't working.

There's lots of hot water.

There's a sofa in the living room.

You've got lots of fresh fruit.

2 You are a guest in A's flat. You want to

- take the dog for a walk
- have a glass of wine
- wash your hair
- watch TV
- use A's car

Ask questions with *Can I …?*

Tapescripts

1.1 Hello Goodbye

A Hello. I'm Sam.
B Oh, hello. I'm Anna.
A Where are you from, Anna?
B I'm from Berlin.

A Hello.
C Oh, hi. I'm Paul. I'm a student here.
A Oh, really? My name's Sam.

A Oh, hi, Lisa. How are you?
D I'm fine. How are you?
A Oh, I'm OK.

A Hello. My name's Sam.
E Hi. I'm John. I'm a teacher here.
A Oh, really? Where are you from?
E I'm from London.

1.2 Photos

This is my car. It's a Citröen, it's very old.
This is my flat. It's very small.
And this is my friend Nina. She's from Italy.
Oh, and this is my friend George. He's from London and he's a student.

2.2 How old are they?

1 My name's André. I'm nine years old, and I'm from Germany.
2 My name's Olga. I'm 16, and I'm from Russia.
3 Hello. My name's Greg. I'm 18 years old, and I'm from the United States.
4 This is Kumiko. She's one year old, and she's from Japan.
5 My name is Caterina. I'm 20, and I'm from Italy.

2.3 Parents and children

1 My name's Paul. I'm married and my wife is a doctor. We have two children. My daughter is 8, and my son is just 3.
2 My name's Isabelle. I'm 19 years old and I'm a student at university. I have one brother – his name's Alan. My mother's a teacher, and my father's a taxi driver.

2.4 Who's who?

A is Donna. She's a police officer, she's 20, she's from Scotland and she has a grey car.
B is James. He's a student, he's 17, he's from Ireland and he has a red car. C is Alice. She's a singer, she's 19, she's from Wales and she has a white car. And D is Bob. He's a waiter, he's 18 years old, he's from England and he has a green car.

Study pages A
Phrasebook: Good morning

1 A Good morning.
   B Good morning. How are you?
   A Fine, thanks.
2 A Good afternoon.
   B Good afternoon.
3 A Good evening, sir.
   B Good evening. Room 315, please.
4 A Good night.
   B Good night. See you tomorrow.

3.1 Sorry

A A Jane – hello. How are you?
   B I'm not Jane, I'm Cathy.
   A Oh – yes, sorry. Cathy, hello. How are you?

B A Excuse me. Two coffees, please.
   B Actually, I'm not a waiter. I'm a customer.
   A Oh, I'm sorry.
C A Oh, good. A taxi. Hello. The Hilton Hotel, please.
   B Sorry. This isn't a taxi. It's my car!
   A Oh, I'm so sorry.
D A Oh, is that your baby? Isn't she lovely? What's her name?
   B He isn't a girl, actually. He's a boy.
   A Oh, of course. Isn't he lovely?
E A So where are you from? New York?
   B No, we aren't American. We're English.
   A Oh, you're English.
   C Yeah, that's right – we're from London.

3.2 Is this seat free?

A Excuse me. Is this your umbrella?
B Oh. Yes, it is. Thanks. Are you a student here?
A Yes. Yes, I am. My name's Mark.
B Hi. I'm Sonia.
A Hi, Sonia. Um, is this seat free?
B Yes, of course.

4.2 Birthday presents

1 A Here's a present for you.
   B Hmm, what is it? ... It's a football! Oh, thank you!
2 A Here you are. Happy birthday.
   B Oh, thanks ... Ooh, a CD. Flamenco music. That's nice. Thank you.
3 A A present for you.
   B Ooh ... It's a jumper! Lovely, thank you!
4 A A present for you. Happy birthday.
   B An umbrella! Thanks.
5 A A present for you. Happy birthday.
   B Mmm ... A watch! Wow! Thank you!
6 A Here you are. Happy birthday.
   B Oh, thanks. Ooh, a lamp! It's lovely! Thank you.

4.4 Precious stones

This is a gold sword, and it's from Istanbul in Turkey. And as you can see, it has lots of diamonds on it, and three very big emeralds.
Now this is a very beautiful brooch. It's from the USA. It has about 100 very small diamonds in it.
And this necklace has rubies and diamonds in it. It's very old, and it's from France.
And this is a very beautiful green bottle. It's from India, and it has red and green stones on it. The red stones are rubies and the green stones are emeralds.

Study pages B
Phrasebook: Excuse me

1 A Ooh, sorry!
   B Oh, that's all right.
   A No, no, I'm sorry – really.
   B It's OK.
2 A Excuse me.
   B Yes?
   A Mr Brown's on the phone.
   B Oh, OK ... Excuse me just a moment.
3 A Excuse me!
   B Yes, sir?
   A A glass of water, please.
   B Certainly, sir.

4 A Excuse me ... Excuse me!
   B Oh, sorry.
   A Thank you.

5.1 Favourite places

1 My favourite place is Penang, in Malaysia. It's very hot, and there are some beautiful beaches. There's a big airport, there are lots of hotels, there are lots of restaurants, and there are lots and lots of tourists.
2 My favourite place is Glenelg in Scotland. It's a very small village – there's just one small shop, there's a church, and that's all. But it's a very beautiful place. It's on the sea, and there are mountains all around.
3 My favourite place is a town called Ouro Preto in Brazil. It's not very big – there are four or five hotels, maybe. But it's a very old town, and there are lots of beautiful old buildings and some beautiful old churches.

6.1 From room to room

A Well, this is the hall – there are two cupboards here, for coats ...
B Oh yes ...
A And here's the living room.
B Oh good – there's a TV.
A Yes, there's a nice sofa too, and a table. And this is a new carpet.
B And that's the balcony?
A Yes, through here. It's a big balcony, again with a table and chairs.
B Mm. Nice place to eat.
A Yes ... Now if we go back through here ... This is the small bedroom – just a bed and a small cupboard here ... and this is the big bedroom through here.
B Oh yes, a nice big bed.
A And there are cupboards here for clothes, and a small TV.
B Great. That's lovely.
A Yeah, it's a nice room. OK, so ... This is the bathroom. Quite small, but there's a bath and a shower, as you can see.
B And the toilet's here.
A Yes, that's right ... OK ... And this is the kitchen. Again, quite small. There's a cooker here, and a fridge, and cupboards of course ... And that's it.

6.3 What's your address?

1 OK, my name's Alison Bailey, that's B-A-I-L-E-Y, OK? And the address is Flat 2, 52 Brighton Road – yes, B-R-I-G-H-T-O-N, Brighton Road, Ealing – E-A-L-I-N-G, and that's London W5 9QT – that's the post code. The phone number is 0181 746 9032.
2 Right. It's Mario Dimambro, D-I-M-A-M-B-R-O, Dimambro. 247 Via Roma – R-O-M-A, Genova – G-E-N-O-V-A, Italy. And the phone number: 656631. That's it.
3 Yes, Philip Denver. Philip – that's P-H-I-L-I-P, one L, and Denver, D-E-N-V-E-R. And it's a thousand and forty nine, 1-0-4-9 Lincoln Drive – L-I-N-C-O-L-N Drive, Boston, 342354, USA. Oh, the telephone? It's 001 – that's for the USA, then 617 584 3921.

6.4 Billionaires

1 Bill Gates's house is on a lake, so you can go there by car or by boat. It's quite big – it has six bedrooms and about 20 other rooms. There's a big dining room, which has seats for about 100 people, and there's also a beautiful library, with lots of old books. The library also has a notebook with writing by Leonardo da Vinci, and that cost more than $30 million. And what's interesting is that there are video screens everywhere – on the walls in all the rooms, even the bathrooms – and these just show pictures – so one day you can have a Picasso, and the next day you can have a Van Gogh, and so on. So it's a nice place, and the rooms have big windows, so you can see the lake and the mountains.

2 The Sultan's Palace is huge – it has nearly 1,800 rooms, 18 lifts, and about 250 toilets. It's huge – very, very big – and some of the rooms are also very big. The dining room, for example, has seats for 4,000 people – that's a big dinner party. And there's also a throne room for the Sultan, and the walls of the throne room are covered in gold, 22-carat gold. And if you want to park your car, there's an underground garage with places for about 700 cars – the Sultan himself has 150 cars, and they're all down under the palace, in the garage.

Study pages C
Phrasebook: Can I have ...?

A Can I have a glass of water, please?
B Yes, of course. Here you are.
A Thank you.

7.1 Free time

1 Well, when I'm on a bus, I usually read a magazine, or sometimes I play a computer game, or maybe listen to music.
2 In my lunchbreak? Oh, sometimes I have a burger – maybe go to the park. Sometimes I play football after lunch.
3 Well, when I'm ill in bed, usually I just read a book, maybe, or watch videos, or if a friend's there, I play cards, maybe.

7.2 Friends

John likes black coffee, I like white.
I like daytime, John likes night.
I like hot showers, he likes cold ones.
I wear new clothes, he wears old ones.

John has short hair, I have long.
I like weak tea, he likes strong.
I wear high heels, he wears low ones.
He likes fast cars, I like slow ones.

Why are we friends? Because, you see,
I like him, but he likes me.

8.1 Food ...

1 We eat a lot of rice – we eat rice every day. We eat a lot of fish, a lot of vegetables, and we eat a lot of fruit.
2 We eat quite a lot of bread, and also rice and beans. We sometimes eat meat. We eat a lot of vegetables and we eat a lot of fruit.
3 We eat a lot of bread, eggs, cheese. We eat a lot of meat, a lot of potatoes and other vegetables. And quite a lot of fruit.
4 We eat a lot of pasta, olive oil, quite a lot of salad and vegetables. But we also eat fish and cheese.

8.3 Waiter!

A Can I have a knife and fork, please?
B I'm very sorry. Yes, of course, sir.
C And I'd like some ketchup, please.
B Ketchup, yes, certainly.

8.4 Fast food

1 A Two cheeseburgers, please ...
   B Two cheeseburgers ...
   A ... and one French fries.
   B Is that small or large?
   A Large, please. And a diet Coke – small.
   B OK. Any dessert?
   A No. That's all, thanks.
   B OK. That's four eighty, please.

2 B Yes please?
   C The hot chilli burger – is that very hot?
   B It's quite hot, yes.
   C OK, I'll have the big burger bonanza then, please.
   B A big burger bonanza. OK ... anything else?
   C Just a cup of coffee, please.
   B OK, that's three twenty, please.

3 B Yes please?
   D The children's meals – what do you get?
   B They come with a small French fries and a small drink.
   D OK, so ...
   E Nuggets and Fanta!
   F Pizza slice and Coke!
   D Two children's meals, please – one chicken nuggets and Fanta, and one pizza slice and Coke.
   B Pizza slice, Coke. Anything else?
   D No, that's all, thanks.
   B OK. Five twenty, please.

Study pages D
Phrasebook: On the phone

1 A Hello. Jane Miller.
   B Hello. Can I speak to George, please?
   A Yes. Just a moment.
   C Hello.
   B Hello, George. It's Mike.
2 A Hello. 26439.
   B Hello. Is Louisa there, please?
   A No, she isn't. Sorry.
   B OK. Never mind.

9.2 What do you do?

A So ... what do you do?
B Oh, I'm a student.
A Oh, yes. What do you study?
B Music.
A Really? I'm a music teacher.
B Are you really? Where do you work, then?
A Oh, at a school, in Cambridge.
B Really? Do you live in Cambridge?
A Yes. Yes, I do. Why, where do you live?
B Cambridge. I live in Cambridge, too.
A Really? Where?
B In Bridge Street – I have a flat in Bridge Street.
A No, that's amazing ...

9.3 From morning till night

Well, I usually get up at a quarter past 7, and then I have breakfast around 8. Then I go to work at half past 8. I start work at a quarter past 9, usually, and I work till half past 12 and then I have lunch. Then I work again in the afternoon, and I always finish work at 5 o'clock. So I get home at 5.30. I have a sandwich then, when I come home, and then I usually have dinner quite late, at about 7 o'clock in the evening. And I go to bed, ooh, at around half past 11, usually.

10.1 At the market

A A Can I see that radio?
   B Yes, here you are.
   A How much is it?
   B £25.
   A Oh no, that's too expensive.
   B All right, 20 then.
B A How much are these lighters?
   B They're £1 each.
   A OK, I'll have one, please.
   B What colour do you want? Red, blue, green?
   A Blue, I think.
   B Here you are, then. That's £1, please.
C A Hello. Can I help you?
   B Yes. What size is that jacket?
   A It's size 38.
   B Oh, that's too big. Thanks anyway.

10.3 Is there a bank near here?

1 A Is there a bank near here?
   B Yes, there's one on the main road, next to the school.
2 A Excuse me, where's the post office?
   B Oh, it's just opposite the station.
3 A Excuse me, is there a supermarket near here?
   B Yes, there's one in Bridge Street, just by the river.
4 A Is there a chemist near here?
   B Yes, let's see ... Yes, there's one on the main road, between the school and the cinema.
5 A Is there a newsagent near here?
   B Yes, there's one in the next street.
6 A Excuse me, is there a good restaurant near here?
   B Yes, there's a very good one near the station – it's called Dino's.
7 A Excuse me, is there a good bookshop near here?
   B No, there isn't, but there's one in the town centre, near the bus station.

10.4 Open and closed

1 In Poland the banks are open till 7 o'clock in the evening. And in towns, supermarkets stay open all night, so you can buy bread at 3 o'clock in the morning.
2 In Greece the shops close at 2 o'clock in the afternoon and open again at 5 o'clock. But there are also lots of kiosks, and they stay open all day.
3 In many cities in Thailand there are large street markets which stay open in the evening. You can buy lots of things there: watches, cameras, books, clothes – lots of things. And they usually stay open till about 12 o'clock at night.

Study pages E
Phrasebook: What does it mean?

1 A What does 'slow' mean?
   B It means 'not fast'.
2 A What does 'millionaire' mean?
   B It's a person who has lots of money.
3 A What's 'amigo' in English?
   B Friend.
4 A What's 'vino' in English?
   B Wine.

11.2 Questions

A Is anyone sitting here?
B Er, no.
A Are you staying at this hotel?
B Yes. Yes, I am.
A What are you reading?
B Excuse me.
A Hey, where are you going?

12.2 Jobs

1 I'm a singer. I sing with a band. I always wear the same thing when I sing – I wear a red jacket and black trousers.
2 Well, I'm a doctor. I work in a large hospital. And I wear a skirt and a blouse and a white coat.
3 I'm a shop assistant. I work in a bookshop. And I usually wear just a jumper and jeans.

12.3 Who do you mean?

1 Anna? She's got blond hair, quite short, and she wears glasses. She's about 25, quite attractive.
2 You know Anna – she drives a blue Volkswagen. She's quite tall, usually wears jeans.
3 You must know Anna – she lives in the next street. She teaches maths, and she's got those two small children.

12.4 Love is all around

I feel it in my fingers, I feel it in my toes. Well, love is all around me, and so the feeling grows.
It's written on the wind, it's everywhere I go. So if you really love me, come on and let it show.

13.2 Shopping list

A Let me see ... We need some orange juice, and some tomatoes, and ... We haven't got any eggs ... What else?
B What about bread?
A No, we've got lots of bread ... Rice? No, we've got rice ... Ah, we haven't got many potatoes.
B Potatoes, OK. What about fruit?
A Oh, yes. Get some apples – and some bananas, maybe. What else? Ah yes, we haven't got any coffee.
B We haven't got much sugar, either.
A OK, sugar. Is that everything?
B I think so, yes.

14.3 What's the weather like?

1 Yes, it's quite warm here, but it's raining ...
2 It's nice and sunny, but it's very windy, and quite cool ...
3 It's very, very cold. And it's snowing ...
4 It's really hot here, quite humid ... No, it isn't sunny at all, it's cloudy, cloudy and very hot ...

Unit 14.4 Festivals

1 Well, we usually go to a party and then at midnight we all go out into the street and we watch fireworks.
2 Well, I usually go out to a restaurant with a lot of friends and we all have a nice meal together and we listen to music and dance and have a good time.
3 I don't do anything. Actually, I don't like New Year's Eve very much, so I go to bed early.
4 Well, we stay at home, but we stay up till midnight and we watch New Year on television.

5 We stay at home till midnight, and then we usually go and visit friends, and we have a few drinks with them.

Study pages G
Focus on ... Can

OK, I can make a cup of coffee, I can make toast, yes ... 'Can you cook rice?' Yes, I can cook rice, no problem ... I can make an omelette, not a very good omelette, but yes, I can make an omelette. Barbecue a chicken ... Yes, I can barbecue a chicken, I can do that. I can't make a cake, no, not really. But I can make my own pasta. I have a pasta machine and I often make my own pasta, yes, so I can do that. But I can't make bread, no.

Study pages G
Phrasebook: Would you like ...?

1 A Would you like an ice-cream?
  B Oh, yes please.
  A OK, what kind?
  B Chocolate.
2 A Hello! Would you like a lift?
  B Oh, yes. Thank you very much.
  A That's OK. Where are you going?
  B Just to the next village.
  A OK.
3 A Would you like another drink?
  B Ooh, yes please.
  A Orange juice, wasn't it?
  B Yes, orange juice with ice.

15.1 Bedtime story

I was about five years old. It was very late at night, and my parents were asleep. I was awake because I wanted to go to the toilet. I went to the toilet, and I saw a light under the living room door. So I opened the door and went in, and I saw a man in the living room. He was about 20 years old.

I looked at him, and he looked at me, and he smiled at me and said, 'Hi! What's your name?' And I said, 'Sam'. 'Do you want to play a game, Sam?' he asked, and I said, 'Yes.' He had a big bag in his hand, and he said, 'OK. Let's put things in this bag.'

So we played the game. I gave things to him, and he put them in his bag. I took my father's wallet out of his jacket, and I took my mother's purse out of her coat, and the man put them in his bag.

Then I went into my parents' bedroom – very quietly – and took their watches and rings, and my mother's earrings, and gave them to the man.

I gave him some other things too – the silver knives, forks and spoons, two clocks and some old books – and he put everything in his bag. It was a great game. And in the end he said, 'OK, Sam. It's bedtime. You go back to bed now. Goodnight.' So I said goodnight and went back to bed.

15.3 Childhood places

1 Our flat was on the third floor, and it was very small – it was really just one room. It had a kitchen and a bathroom, but they were very, very small – they were like cupboards, really. The room had one big window, and outside there was a small balcony. And in the room there were two sofas, one on each side. And at night these sofas were our beds – my parents slept in one, and I slept in the other with my little sister.

2 I remember my grandmother's house, where I stayed every summer. It was in the country, and it was quite small – it only had a living room and two bedrooms – but it had a really big garden, and there were lots of trees, and it was very quiet. It was an old house, and it had lovely old wooden furniture. And I remember there was a large veranda which went all round the house, so there was always a sunny place to sit. I loved it.

16.3 Which country?

1 India – well, it's a large country, very large. It's also a very poor country, at least most people are poor. What else? It's in Asia ... The capital is New Delhi, I think, and the River Ganges flows through it. It's very hot in the summer and the winter, I think – but not in the north, of course. In the north there are mountains, very high mountains – the Himalayas.
2 What do I know about Switzerland? Well, it's in Europe, in the centre of Europe, it isn't on the sea. It has a lot of lakes, and a lot of mountains – it's very cold in the winter. It's a very rich country – a very beautiful country as well. And there are three main languages, I think – French, German and Italian.
3 Argentina is in South America, and people speak Spanish there. It's a very big country. The south of the country is very cold – I'm not sure about the north, but the south is certainly cold. And the capital is Buenos Aires.

16.4 International travel

1 B Good morning.
  A Good morning.
  B Could I see your ticket and passport, please? ... Thank you. Just one bag to check in, is it?
  A Yes, just one.
  B OK ... Would you like a smoking or a non-smoking seat?
  A Non-smoking, please, by the window.
  B A window seat, OK. There you are.
  A Thank you.
  B Thank you. Have a good flight.
2 Ladies and gentlemen, welcome to Miami, where the time is exactly 3.20 in the afternoon. We hope you had a good flight and ...
3 A Miami Beach Hotel, please.
  C Miami Beach Hotel. OK.
4 D Good afternoon.
  A Hello. You've got a room reserved for Brown.
  D Mrs Brown – just a moment ... Yes, here we are, ma'am. Three nights, is that right?
  A Yes, that's right.
  D OK ... Your room number is 926. It's on the ninth floor. Here's your key, ma'am.
  A Thank you.
5 A Hello? Richard? It's me, Karen.
  E Karen, hi. Are you in Miami? Did you have a good flight?
  A Yes, fine. Is everything OK? How are the children?
  E Oh, they're fine. They're both asleep. What's it like there? Is it hot?
  A Yes, it is. Sunny and very hot. What's it like in London?
  E Oh, still raining.

A OK, look. I'll phone again tomorrow. OK?
E OK. Bye.
6 F Room service. Can I help you?
A Yes, I'd like a chicken sandwich, please.
F Yes, ma'am. Anything to drink?
A Yes, a cold beer, please.
F OK. What's your room number?
A 926.
F 926. Fine. Thank you.

Study pages H
Focus on … Dates
My name's Henry. My birthday's on 1st March.
My name's André. My birthday's on 26th July.
My name's Hazel, and my birthday is 22nd April.
OK, my name's Chris, and my birthday is 9th June.
Hello, my name's Natasha, and my birthday's on 26th December.
My name is Gabi, and my birthday is on 20th February.

Study pages H
Phrasebook: I'm not sure
A What's the capital of India?
B I think it's Bombay.

A What is the capital of India?
C I don't know. Is it Calcutta?

A What's the capital of India?
D I have no idea. Sorry.

A What is the capital of India?
E I'm not sure, but I think it's Delhi.

17.2 Did you see …?
1 A Did you see that programme about hospitals last night?
 B Yes, I did.
 A Did you like it?
 B Yes, I did. It was quite interesting.
2 A Did you watch the football match on Sunday?
 B No, I didn't. Was it good?
 A Yes, it was. We won 2–0.
3 A Did you go to the concert yesterday?
 B No. Did you?
 A Yes, I did.
 B Did you enjoy it?
 A No, it was really boring.

17.3 Memory test
A OK, can you remember your first day at school?
B My first day at school …
A What did you wear?
B I wore … I don't know. Jeans and a T-shirt, probably, but I don't really remember.
A OK, and what was your teacher's name?
B Oh, I remember that. It was Mr Fish.
A Mr Fish?
B Yes.
A Can you remember your first day at school?
C Yes, I think so.
A OK, what did you wear?
C I wore a dress, a summer dress – it was a very hot day, and I wore a red and white dress.
A What was your teacher's name?
C My first teacher? Mrs … Mrs Grey, I think.

18.1 From A to B
Well, the prisoner climbs through the window on to the balcony, and then he climbs down the rope. Then he goes along the path until he comes to the hut. Then he goes into the hut, and he goes down the ladder, and then down the second ladder. Then he goes down the steps, and he goes across the bridge, and he goes on until he comes to the lake. Then he gets into the boat and goes across the lake. When he reaches the other side, he climbs up the tree. Then he goes through a short tunnel, climbs up the ladder and climbs over the wall – and he's free.

18.3 It's on the left
1 You come out of the station and turn right into King Street. Then you turn left into this little road here, and the cinema's at the end, just here on the corner of Canal Street. OK?
2 OK. You get off the bus here, opposite the bridge. Then you go across the river and just carry straight on – you're in Bridge Street now, so just carry on along Bridge Street and you come to a church. Go past the church and turn right, and the house is just along there.

18.4 The island of Odysseus
Most people go to Greece by plane. So if you fly into Athens, first of all you need to get down to Patras. So you take a bus or a train down to Patras. That takes three or four hours. Then you can take a ferry boat that calls in at Kefalonia and then goes to Ithaki, and that takes maybe four or five hours.

You can also fly in to Kefalonia, there's an airport on Kefalonia. But there aren't any buses at the airport, so you have to take a taxi. You take a taxi right across the island, and that takes maybe 45 minutes or an hour. And then from there you can take a ferry over to Ithaki, and that takes about one hour.

A lot of people drive down to Greece, and you can get a ferry across to Greece from Italy, which takes about 24 hours, about one day. And then you get off the ferry at Igoumenitsa, drive down the coast for two or three hours, and then you can get a ferry across to Ithaki.

So that's three ways of getting to Ithaki.

Study pages I
Phrasebook: Let's …
1 A Let's get some petrol.
 B Yes, that's a good idea.
2 A Shall we dance?
 B No, I don't want to just at the moment.
3 A Let's ask for the bill.
 B Not yet. I'd like another drink.
4 A Shall we take a taxi?
 B No. Let's walk.

19.2 Can I …?
1 A Can I use the phone?
 B Of course. It's in the hall.
2 A Can I smoke?
 C No, sorry, you can't, not in here. But you can smoke on the balcony.
3 A Can I listen to the news?
 B Yes, of course you can. There's a radio in the kitchen.
4 A Can I have a glass of beer?
 C Sorry, we haven't got any beer. You can have fruit juice, or lemonade.

19.3 All in a day's work
1 I work as a cleaner in a big hotel. It's not a very nice job. I have to get up very early – I get up at about 5 o'clock, and I start work at 6. And some of the people are friendly, but not all of them – of course I always have to be polite, and that's quite difficult sometimes. One good thing is, I don't have to work long hours – I finish at about 10 in the morning, and then I can go home.
2 Well, I work on a fishing boat. It's a hard job, and it's quite dangerous too. You have to be very careful when the weather's bad. We go out to sea for about three or four weeks usually, so I have to be away from home a lot. The good thing about it – about the only good thing – the money's very good, so I don't have to work all year – I work about six months, usually, and that's good enough to live on.
3 I work in an Italian restaurant in London – I'm a waitress. And it's quite a nice job, I like it. I have to be nice to everyone and smile a lot, of course, but people are usually friendly anyway, so that's not a problem. I have to work late in the evening, usually till about 11 or 12 at night. But then I don't have to get up early because I don't work in the morning.

20.2 Are you an athlete?
'Can you run 100 metres?' Yes, I can do that. And run five kilometres … no. 'Can you swim 100 metres?' Yes, I can swim 100 metres, but I can't swim one kilometre. Can I ride a bike? Yes. Can I ride a bike with no hands? No, I don't think so. Climb up a ladder, yes. Climb up a rope? Yes, I can do that. Jump over a stream one metre wide? I can, that's easy. Jump over a wall one metre high? No, I can't do that. Catch a tennis ball in one hand is easy. Throw a tennis ball 50 metres? No, I can't do that. 'Can you kick a football 100 metres?' No, I can't do that. 'Can you stand on your head?' No! And 'Can you walk on your hands?' No.

20.4 I did it!
First you have to pay, and it's quite expensive – I paid £40 for just one jump. And then you put on a harness. And the harness goes round your body, and down your legs to your feet. And then you walk up to the cage. The cage is quite big – big enough for five or six people – and there's this very long piece of elastic. The elastic is very thick, very strong, and one end of the elastic is fixed under the cage, and they fix the other end of the elastic to your harness.

OK, then you get in the cage, and it starts to go up. And it goes up really high – about 60 metres. And when you look down, everything's very small down there, all the people are very small.

And then the man opens the door of the cage. And you think 'I don't want to do this. This is crazy.' But the man says 'OK, you go when I count to three.' And he counts to three – one, two, three – and you jump.

And it's all very quick – you fall very quickly – then the elastic pulls you up again, and you go up and down, up and down, and then you stop, and you just hang there. And then the cage comes down slowly, slowly brings you down to the ground, and that's it. You take off your harness. And they give you a certificate, and the certificate says 'I did it!'.

Study pages J
Phrasebook: Could you ...?

A Could you bring me some fruit?
B Yes, of course.
A And could you buy me a bottle of beer?
B No, sorry, I can't do that.

21.2 Which is better?

A I'd like a small camera, for a child. It's my daughter. She's 10.
B OK. We've got this one. This is a Yashica. Or there's this one – a Canon.
A Which is better?
B Well, the Canon is a better camera, really. But maybe the Yashica is better for a child – it's very easy to use.
A Which is cheaper?
B The Yashica's cheaper – it's £40. And the Canon's £70.
A OK. I'll have the Yashica, please.

22.1 Going out

Yes, I visit my friends a lot at the weekend, and relatives – I see my brother quite often, and his family. And I often go out for a drink, almost every Saturday, in fact. I don't go out for meals so much. And I don't go for a walk usually, no. I never go for a bike ride. And I don't go shopping, not for fun, anyway – I don't like shopping. But I go to the cinema a lot – not concerts, not sports events, but the cinema, certainly. I don't do much sport, really – I go swimming sometimes, but not very often. And I don't drive, I haven't got a car. But most weekends I go fishing, usually on Sunday if the weather's nice.

22.4 The curse of the new ground

United were one of the best football teams in the country. They had a lot of supporters, but their ground wasn't very big. They wanted to move to a bigger ground. So they bought some land on the edge of the city. There was nothing on this land except for one small cottage. An old woman lived in this cottage. 'We're sorry,' the club told her, 'but you have to go. We want to build a new stadium on this land.' The woman said no, so the police came and moved her. But as she left, she shouted, 'United will never win a match on this land! Remember my words!'

They started to build the new stadium, but they had lots of problems. One of the walls fell down, and two workers died in strange accidents. In the end, they finished the stadium, and 40,000 supporters came to watch the first match. United lost the match 5–0. That season, United won lots of matches in other football grounds. But they lost all the matches they played at home. The next year, the same thing happened. The team's manager left, and a new one came – but it made no difference. United lost all their home matches.

So now United Football Club want to sell the ground and find a new one. But there's one big problem: who wants to buy a football ground with a curse on it?

Study pages K
Focus on ... Verb + to

1 A Do you want to come to the cinema this evening?
  B No, sorry. I'd like to come, but I have to do my homework.
2 A Would you like to go and see a film this evening?
  C Oh no, thanks. There's a football match on, and I want to watch it.
3 A Do you want to go to the cinema tonight?
  D Yes, fine.
  A Would you like to go for a drink first?
  D OK. I need to wash my hair. But I can meet you at about 6.30.

Study pages K
Phrasebook: What did you say?

1 A So where are you living at the moment, then?
  B Sorry, what did you say?
  A I said, where are you living?
  B Oh – in London.
2 C That's a lovely dress you're wearing there.
  B Sorry, could you say that again?
  C I said, that's a lovely dress. Your dress is lovely.
  B Oh, thank you.
3 D So are you a student here, then, or what?
  B Sorry, I don't understand.
  D Are you a student?
  B Yes. Yes, I'm a student.

23.1 I love Paris

1 I'm going to go shopping. I'm going to buy clothes and shoes, probably, and I'm also going to visit the Louvre. And in the evening I'm going to meet some friends, and we're going to have dinner together in a nice restaurant.
2 Well, I'm on business here, and I'm going to stay in a hotel in the centre of Paris, but I've got some free time too, so if I have time I'm going to visit some art galleries, maybe some museums. And in the evening I'm going to go to the theatre.
3 Well, we're going to stay with friends here, and we're just going to relax, really. We're going to walk around the streets, sit in cafés, you know, drink coffee ... And in the evening, we're going to go to a café or a club, probably, and listen to music.

23.3 Help!

A Hi, look, I'm painting my living room on Saturday ...
B Oh yes ...
A Could you help me?
B Sorry. I'm working on Saturday.
A Oh. What about Sunday?
B No, I'm seeing friends on Sunday. Sorry.

A Is that John?
C Yes.
A Oh, John, hi, it's Paul here.
C Oh, hi, Paul.
A I'm painting my living room this weekend. Could you help me?
C No, sorry. I can't. I'm playing football on Saturday ...
A What about ...?
C ... and on Sunday I'm going swimming. Sorry.

24.1 I'm hungry!

1 A Are you all right?
  B No. I feel really ill.
  A Oh dear. Shall I phone the doctor?
2 A Oh, I'm tired.
  B Why don't you lie down and have a rest?
3 A I'm really hungry.
  B Why don't you have a sandwich? There's some cheese in the fridge.
  A OK.
4 A I'm hot.
  B Me too. Let's have a swim.
  A Yeah. Good idea.
5 A I feel a bit cold.
  B Why don't you put on a jumper?
6 A I feel thirsty.
  B OK. Let's go to a café and have something to drink
  A Mm.

24.3 Did you enjoy it?

1 Well I saw *Titanic*, and yes, I really enjoyed it, it was really exciting. It was also quite sad, I thought, but ... really good.
2 Yes, I saw *Titanic*. It wasn't very good – it was quite exciting, I suppose, but much too long, and the actors weren't very good.
3 I saw a *Mr Bean* video. It was OK, some parts were very funny and ... but some parts were quite boring as well. I enjoyed it.
4 I saw a *Mr Bean* video. I thought it was really funny – I enjoyed it a lot.

24.4 Showing your feelings

Paul Elkman is an American scientist. He wanted to know the answer to this question: Do people show feelings in the same way everywhere in the world?

Ekman took photos of people in the USA. Some people looked happy, some looked sad, some looked angry, some looked surprised, and some looked frightened. He showed the photos to people from 21 countries, and asked them to match the feelings with the faces. He found that everyone could do this quite easily: everyone agreed which people were happy, which were sad, which were angry, and so on.

Then Ekman went to a village in Papua New Guinea. In this village, people had no television, they saw no films, and they never saw people from other countries. So they didn't know what people from other countries looked like. Ekman showed his photos to the people in this village, and asked them the same questions: Which people are happy? Which are sad? Which are angry? He found that even here they could answer the questions quite easily.

So Ekman's conclusion was that people do show feelings in the same way everywhere in the world.

Reference section

1 People and places

Verb *to be*

Long form	Short form
I am	I'm
You are	You're
He/She is	He's/She's
We are	We're
They are	They're

He My brother's a student.
He's a student.

She My mother's a doctor.
She's a doctor.

It This car is a Rolls Royce.
It's a Rolls Royce.

They  My friends are students.
They're students.

You can be singular or plural:

How are you?
I'm fine, thanks

How are you?
We're fine, thanks.

Questions		*Answers*
What's your name?	→	(It's) Bill.
How are you?	→	I'm fine (thanks).
Where are you from?	→	(I'm from) Japan.

Countries

 Britain the USA Spain Japan

 France Germany Italy Brazil

 Russia Australia

Useful vocabulary

teacher	flat	small	hello
student	office	old	goodbye
friend	car	this	I don't know

2 In the family

Singular and plural

To make a plural, add *-s*:

a boy → boys   a bird → birds   a car → cars

-y changes to *-ies*:

a baby → babies   a family → families

Note:
child → children

Verb *to have*

I have	We have
You have	They have
He/she has	

Numbers 1–20

1 one	6 six	11 eleven	16 sixteen
2 two	7 seven	12 twelve	17 seventeen
3 three	8 eight	13 thirteen	18 eighteen
4 four	9 nine	14 fourteen	19 nineteen
5 five	10 ten	15 fifteen	20 twenty

Families

wife ↔ husband
mother / father
daughter / son
sister ↔ brother

Useful vocabulary

boy	child	dog	doctor	taxi driver
girl	children	cat	university	
baby	family	bird	married	

Study pages A

The English alphabet

Aa Bb Cc Dd Ee Ff Gg Hh Ii Jj Kk Ll Mm
Nn Oo Pp Qq Rr Ss Tt Uu Vv Ww Xx Yy Zz

A, E, I, O, U are *vowels*. The others are *consonants*.
Y can be either a vowel (*baby*) or a consonant (*yes*).

my, your, his, her

I → my
you → your
he → his
she → her

I'm a student.   This is my flat.
How are you?   What's your name?
He's English.   His wife is Italian.
She's 18.   Her brother's 15.

3 To be or not to be?

Verb *to be*

Negative
To make the negative, add *not* or *n't*:
They are here.   They aren't here.
This is my car.   This isn't my car.

Long form	Short form
I am not	I'm not
You are not	You aren't
He/She is not	He/She isn't
We are not	We aren't
You are not	You aren't
They are not	They aren't

Questions
To make a question, change the word order:
$\overset{1}{\text{They}}$ $\overset{2}{\text{are}}$ here. $\overset{1}{\text{Are}}$ $\overset{2}{\text{they}}$ here?
$\overset{1}{\text{This}}$ $\overset{2}{\text{is}}$ my car. $\overset{1}{\text{Is}}$ $\overset{2}{\text{this}}$ your car?

> Are you 18?
> Is he from the USA?
> Are they married?

Wh- questions

Where is she?	She's in Paris.
What's that?	It's my car.
Who's that?	It's my son.
How old is he?	He's seven.
How is your wife?	She's fine.

Useful vocabulary

waiter	seat	coffee
customer	free	these
England	café	thanks

4 Things around you

Colours

red   green   black   grey
blue   orange   white   brown
yellow   pink

Light and dark colours
light blue   light green   light brown
dark blue   dark green   dark brown

Things in rooms

Where is it?

The lamp is *on* the table.
The picture is *behind* the lamp.
The bag is *under* the table.
The shoes are *by* the door.

Questions	Answers
Where's the bag?	It's under the table.
Where are my shoes?	They're by the door.

Useful vocabulary

face	tree	book	jumper
hair	watch	camera	umbrella
sky	football	shoes	glasses
mountain	ring	bag	pen

Study pages B

Numbers 20–100

20	twenty	50	fifty	80	eighty
30	thirty	60	sixty	90	ninety
40	forty	70	seventy	100	a hundred

21	twenty-one	34	thirty-four	47	forty-seven
22	twenty-two	35	thirty-five	48	forty-eight
23	twenty-three	36	thirty-six	49	forty-nine

a and *an*

We use *a* before consonants:
a table   *a* window   *a* hundred
We use *an* before vowels (*a, e, i, o, u*):
an umbrella   *an* address book

this, that, these, those

this   these   that   those

Sorry and *Excuse me*

Sorry!   Excuse me!   Excuse me!

5 There's …

There is and There are

Use:
- *There is* (or *There's*) and *There isn't* + singular
- *There are* and *There aren't* + plural

There's a café in the village.

There isn't an airport here.

There are three cafés in the village.

There aren't any good restaurants.

Questions

To make questions, change the word order:

There is a café near here.   Is there a café near here?

There are two good hotels.   Are there any good hotels?

some and any

some:	There are some good bookshops here.
any:	There aren't any good bookshops here.
	Are there any good bookshops here?

How many?

 How many floors are there?

 How many people are there?

Useful vocabulary

place	building	lift	TV
shop	floor	toilet	town
hotel	swimming pool	tourist	village
restaurant	car park	beautiful	airport
church	stairs	library	favourite
beach			

6 Where you live

Things in the home

living room   bedroom

kitchen   bathroom

1	sofa	5	cupboard	9	clock
2	TV	6	cooker	10	bath
3	carpet	7	fridge	11	shower
4	single bed	8	shelf	12	mirror

Where?

 There's a plant in the corner.

 Where's the phone? It's by the door.

 The radio is on the shelf.

 There are two pictures on the wall.

Name and address

First name: *Carole*   City: *Cambridge*

Last name: *Jones*   Post code: *CB26 3JY*

Street: *55 Kings Road*   Country: *England*

Phone number: *01223 049584*

Study pages C

Possessives

I	→ my	This is my daughter.
you	→ your	Is this your bag?
he	→ his	His first name is Robert.
she	→ her	Her phone number is 260375.
we	→ our	This is our bedroom.
they	→ their	What's their address?

With nouns, add *'s*:

my father	→ my father's	This my father's car.
Maria	→ Maria's	Are you Maria's brother?

Note: 's has two meanings:

I'm Maria's brother (= I'm her brother).

Maria's at home (= Maria is at home).

First, second, third …

1st	first	5th	fifth	8th	eighth
2nd	second	6th	sixth	9th	ninth
3rd	third	7th	seventh	10th	tenth
4th	fourth				

What's your first name?   It's her tenth birthday

My flat is on the sixth floor.   He's their third child.

Can I have…?

Can I have	a glass of water that book	please?

Yes, (of course). Here you are.	Thank you.

7 Things people do

Present simple (verb: *to speak*)

I speak You speak We speak They speak	English.

He She	speaks English.

After *he/she/it* or a noun, add *-s*:
She listens to jazz.
Our teacher plays the guitar.

Negative
To make the negative, use *don't* or *doesn't* + verb:

I don't You don't We don't They don't	speak English.

He She	doesn't speak English.

Note: After *don't/doesn't*, the verb stays the same:
I don't wear jeans. → He doesn't wear jeans.
(*not* ~~He doesn't wears~~ ...)

Verbs

go (to the shops)
have (a sandwich)
listen (to music)
look (out of the window)
play (cards, football)
read (a magazine)
watch (TV)
live (in London)

like (cars, music)
wear (jeans, glasses)
smoke (cigarettes)
eat (meat, pizza)
drink (coffee)
talk (to a friend)
speak (English)

Adjectives

high   low
hot   cold
fast   slow

new   old
short   long
strong weak

8 Food and drink

Basic food

rice   oil   cheese   meat   fruit   beans
bread   pasta eggs   fish   vegetables   potatoes

Drinks

water   lemonade   tea   wine   milk
fruit juice Coca-Cola   coffee   beer   milk shake

I	often sometimes never	drink tea.

I drink tea every day.

Things on the table

plate   knife   salt
glass   fork   pepper
cup   spoon   sugar

Asking for things

Can I have	a glass of water a knife	please?

I'd like	a Coca-cola a plate	please.

---

9 Do you…?

Present simple questions

To make questions, use *do* or *does* + verb:

Do you Do they	like music?

Does he Does she	like music?

Note: After *do/does*, the main verb stays the same:

Do you go to school?   →   Does he go to school?
(not ~~Does he goes~~ …?)

Questions	*Short answers*
Do you eat meat?	Yes, I *do*. No, I *don't*.
Do they live here?	Yes, they *do*. No, they *don't*.
Does she have a car?	Yes, she *does*. No, she *doesn't*.
Does your father smoke?	Yes, he *does*. No, he *doesn't*.

Wh- questions

Where do they live?	(They live) in Cairo.
When do you go to school?	At 8 o'clock.
What does he do?	He's a bus driver.
What does she study?	(She studies) English.

Everyday activities

get up	start work		breakfast
go to bed	finish work	have	lunch
go to work/school	come home		dinner

Other new verbs

keep (a diary)	carry (a bag)
sleep	study (English)

10 Things people buy

Shopping

Questions		*Answers*
Can I see that camera?	→	Yes, here you are.
How much is that jumper?	→	It's £35.50.
What size are these shoes?	→	They're size 34.

Shops and things they sell

butcher	meat (beef, lamb, pork, chicken)
chemist	medicines, sun cream, toothpaste
bookshop	books
newsagent	newspapers, magazines, pens, paper
kiosk	ice-cream, cigarettes, drinks, magazines
baker	bread, cakes
greengrocer	vegetables, fruit
clothes shop	clothes

Other places in towns

supermarket	restaurant	cinema	station	bank
post office	café		school	hotel

Place prepositions

The café is *by* the river.   It's *opposite* the school.
It's *next to* the cinema.   It's *near* the station.
It's *between* the cinema *and* the river.

Other useful vocabulary

aspirin	T-shirt	expensive	Can I help you?
sunglasses	map	too (big)	

Study pages E

Days of the week

Monday	Friday
Tuesday	Saturday
Wednesday	Sunday
Thursday	

To talk about days, use *on*:

They go to church *on* Sunday.
I go to work *on* Monday morning.
We usually go to the cinema *on* Saturday evening.

Kilos and litres

5 kg = five kilos	five kilos of apples
1 kg = a kilo	a kilo of rice
0.5 kg = half a kilo	half a kilo of sugar
100 g = a hundred grams	a hundred grams of cheese
1 l = a litre	a litre of milk
0.5 l = half a litre	half a litre of wine

I like and *I'd like*

I like = I think it's nice	I'd like = I want
I like ice-cream.	It's hot! *I'd like* an ice-cream.
I like dogs.	*I'd like* a dog for my birthday.
I like coffee.	*I'd like* a cup of coffee, please.

11 What's going on?

Present simple and Present continuous

There are two ways to talk about the present in English: Present simple and Present continuous.

Present simple (= usually, every day)
Philippe *works* in a bank.
He *goes* to work at 8.30
and he *comes* home at 5.00.

Present continuous (= now)
Today is a holiday. Philippe *isn't working*. *He's sitting* on his balcony and *he's reading* the newspaper.

Present continuous

To form the Present continuous, use *be* + verb + *-ing*:

I'm He's/She's They're	reading.	I'm not He/She isn't They aren't	reading.

Are you Is he/she Are they	listening?	What are you doing? Where are you staying? Where is she going?

Activity verbs

wash (the dishes)	dance	read (a book)
clean (your teeth)	cook (a meal)	write (a letter)
have (a shower)	play (the piano)	listen to (the radio)
make (coffee)	watch (TV)	

Where is he?

He's asleep. (= he's sleeping)
He's out. (= he isn't at home)
He's away for the weekend. (= he isn't in this town)
He's at home.
He's at school.
He's at a friend's flat.

Other useful vocabulary

sit	football match	do your homework
anyone	at the moment	I'm afraid

12 Describing people

Clothes

He's wearing …  … a jacket, jeans and a jumper.	He's wearing … … a coat, a hat and trousers.	She's wearing … … a skirt and a blouse.
She's wearing …  … shorts and a T-shirt.	He's wearing …  … a suit, a shirt and a tie.	She's wearing …  … a dress.

Some clothes are plural: *trousers, jeans, shorts*.
We can also say *a pair of trousers, a pair of jeans, a pair of shorts* (but not ~~a trouser, a shorts~~).

Names of jobs

doctor	singer	engineer	shop assistant
student	waiter	secretary	

We can also say:

I work *in*	a bank. an office.	I work *for*	a large company. Esso.

Appearance

He's/She's	tall. short.	He/She has	long short	dark fair grey	hair.

Other useful vocabulary

band	drive (a car)	insurance company
hospital	French	

Study pages F

Imperatives

To form imperatives, simply use the basic verb:

Look!	Open the window, please.
Listen!	Give me that book.
Come here!	Put it on the table.

To make the negative, add *Don't*:

Don't look!	Please don't open the window.
Don't talk so much	Don't eat sweets.

Expressions with *have*

lunch · breakfast · a bath · dinner · a shower · **HAVE** · a sandwich · a sleep · a drink · a good time · a party

13 How much?

Count and non-count nouns

Some nouns in English have a singular and a plural – these are called *count nouns* (because we can count them):

a cup   four cups   a potato   potatoes

Some nouns have only a singular form – these are called *non-count nouns*. We don't use *a* or *an* with them:

paper   water   gold

Some common non-count nouns

rice   water   paper   meat   coffee   food   bread
sugar   beer   money   fruit   tea   oil   cheese

Quantity expressions

Use *many* with count nouns, and *much* with non-count nouns. Use *some*, *lots of* and *any* with all nouns.

Count	Non-count
We've got *lots of* eggs.	We've got *lots of* tea.
We haven't got *many* eggs.	We haven't got *much* tea.
We haven't got *any* eggs.	We haven't got *any* tea.
How many eggs are there?	*How much* tea is there?

have got

I've got = I have got. He's got = He has got. They mean the same as *I have, He has.* We use this form especially in spoken English.

I've got She's got They've got	a car.	I haven't got He hasn't got They haven't got	a car.

Other useful vocabulary

envelope   bowl   matches   jam
key   soap   blood   light a fire

14 Around the year

Seasons

spring   summer   autumn   winter
wet season   dry season

Adjectives

wet   hot   warm   humid
dry   cold   cool

Temperature

$40°$ = forty degrees
$0°$ = zero
$-10°$ = minus ten degrees (*or* ten degrees below zero)

Months

January	April	July	October
February	May	August	November
March	June	September	December

To talk about months and seasons, use *in*:

We usually go on holiday *in July*.
What's the weather like *in December*?
It usually snows here *in (the) winter*.

The weather

It's   It's   It's   It's   It's
raining snowing sunny   cloudy   windy

Talking about the weather
It's lovely weather today.
The weather isn't very nice.
What's the weather like?

Other useful vocabulary

night   Christmas   holiday

Study pages G

Can

Positive and negative forms:

I He/She They	can can't	play the piano.

Questions

Can you Can he	play the piano?

Numbers over 100

100 a hundred   101 a hundred and one
200 two hundred   120 a hundred and twenty
300 three hundred   121 a hundred and twenty-one
1,000 a thousand
2,000 two thousand
3,000 three thousand
100,000   a hundred thousand
1,000,000 a million

15 In the past 1

Past simple

Regular verbs
To make the Past simple, add *-ed* or *-d*.
play → played   want → wanted   live → lived
look → looked   listen → listened   like → liked

I played He/She played They played	football yesterday.

Irregular verbs

give	gave	have	had
take	took	say	said
put	put	read	read (/red/)
see	saw	write	wrote
go	went	buy	bought

See also the list of irregular verbs on page 127.

Verb to be

I was You were He/She was We were They were	at home yesterday.

Time expressions

on	*days*: *on* Saturday.
in	*months*: *in* September, *in* July *seasons*: *in* the winter, *in* the spring *years*: *in* 1969
at	*times*: *at* 6 o'clock, *at* the weekend

Useful vocabulary

smile	light	wallet	yesterday
want	game	purse	quiet
late	thing	silver	garden

16 Around the world

North, south, east, west

He lives *in the north* of England.
The mountains are *in the east*.
It's a large town *on the west coast*.

Kinds of town

I live in a large *town*, but my parents live in a small *village* in the country.
Cairo is the *capital* of Egypt. It is a huge *city*, with more than 15 million people.
They stayed at a ski *resort* in the Alps.
Yokohoma is in Japan. It is also a large *sea port*.

Where is it?

It's …   *on* the sea   *on* a river   *in* the mountains
          on the coast   *on* a lake

Continents

Countries and languages

Country	Language	Country	Language
–	Arabic	Japan	Japanese
China	Chinese	Poland	Polish
France	French	Portugal	Portuguese
Germany	German	Russia	Russian
Greece	Greek	Spain	Spanish
Italy	Italian	Turkey	Turkish

Other useful vocabulary

island   holiday   love (v.)   ferry   visit

Study pages H

Ordinal numbers

11th eleventh	**21st** twenty-first
12th twelfth	**22nd** twenty-second
13th thirteenth	**23rd** twenty-third
14th fourteenth	**24th** twenty-fourth
15th fifteenth	**25th** twenty-fifth
20th twentieth	**30th** thirtieth

Dates

1st July = the first of July
30th September = the thirtieth of September
22nd April = the twenty-second of April
3rd May = the third of May

Verbs with indirect objects

We can say:

He	wrote sent gave	a letter to me.

He	wrote sent gave	me a letter.

Other examples:
I showed *her* my passport. (not ~~I showed to her~~ …)
They sent *us* some money.
Can you bring *me* some water, please?
She gave *him* a watch for his birthday.

17 In the past 2

Past simple

Negative
To form the Past simple negative, use *didn't* + verb:

I went She went	to the concert last night.

I didn't go She didn't go	to the concert last night.

Questions
To make Past simple questions, use *did* + verb:

Did you go Did she go	to the concert?

Note: After *did* and *didn't*, the main verb is in the infinitive form, not the past:

She *played* tennis → She didn't *play* tennis
They *saw* the film → Did they *see* the film ?

was and *were*

Negatives

He wasn't They weren't	at home.

Questions

Was he Were they	at home?

Irregular verbs

make made   wear wore   win won   eat ate
get got   cost cost   leave left

See also the list of irregular verbs, page 127.

Other useful vocabulary

paint	die	programme	interesting
start	war	football match	boring
arrive	play (n.)	concert	fireworks

18 How to get there

Direction

go *along* the road   go *across/over* the bridge   climb *over* the wall

go *into* the house   come *out of* the house   go *past* the house

go *up* the steps   go *down* the steps   climb *through* the window

Giving directions

← Turn left   ⤵ Turn right   ↑ Go Carry : straight on

Transport

go by train   go by bus   go by taxi

drive (go by car)   cycle (go by bike)   walk (go on foot)

Other useful vocabulary

ladder	path	bus stop	tunnel
hut	rope	at the end	on the corner

Study pages I

Short answers

To give short answers, repeat the auxiliary verb (*is*, *was*, *can*, *does*, *did*, etc.).

Are you from Mexico?	Yes, I *am*.	No, I'm *not*.
Is she a teacher?	Yes, she *is*.	No, she *isn't*.
Is there a café here?	Yes, there *is*.	No, there *isn't*.
Are they working?	Yes, they *are*.	No, they *aren't*.
Was your father here?	Yes, he *was*.	No, he *wasn't*.
Can you sing?	Yes, I *can*.	No, I *can't*.
Does Carl smoke?	Yes, he *does*.	No, he *doesn't*.
Did you have a bath?	Yes, I *did*.	No, I *didn't*.

Let's ... and *Shall we ...?*

Let's go to the cinema. Shall we go to the cinema?	That's a good idea.
	No, thanks. I don't want to.

Years

We usually say years in 'pairs' of numbers:
1924 = 19 24 = nineteen twenty-four
1848 = 18 48 = eighteen forty-eight
But:
1900 = nineteen hundred   2000 = two thousand
2001 = two thousand and one

19 You mustn't do that!

must and mustn't

You must … = Do it!

You must show your passport.
You must stay in bed.

You mustn't … = Don't do it!

You mustn't take photographs.
You mustn't get out of bed.

can and can't

Ability	Permission
He *can* speak Thai …	We *can* watch TV…
… but he *can't* speak German.	… but we *can't* play loud music.
– *Can* you swim?	– *Can* I go, please?
– Yes, I *can*.	– No, you *can't*!

Note: After *must* and *can* we do not use *to*:

You *must stay* here. (not ~~You must to stay~~ …)
We *can't use* the phone. (not ~~We can't to use~~ …)

have to and don't have to

I have to He has to	work hard.	I don't have to He doesn't have to	work hard.

I have to = I must do it, it's necessary:
I have to get up early during the week (because I start work at 7.30).

I don't have to = It isn't necessary:
I don't have to get up early at weekends (I can stay in bed late if I want to).

Useful vocabulary

gun	take a photo	hard	cleaner (n.)
stop (v.)	polite	dangerous	fishing boat
animals	careful		

20 The body

Parts of the body

HEAD
eye hair
nose ear
neck mouth

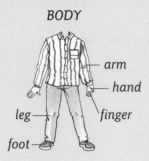
BODY
arm
hand
leg finger
foot

Adjectives

long	thin	large *or* big	wide
short	fat	small	narrow

She has a narrow face and a long thin nose.

He has a wide face, a short nose and a small mouth.

Action verbs

stand	walk	run	jump

climb	swim	catch	throw

kick	ride	drive	fly

Other useful vocabulary

careful	friendly	in the middle	metre
stream	human	at the top	kilometre

Study pages J

Adjectives and adverbs

Adjectives go with nouns, or after the verb *to be*:
Their *house* is very *quiet*.
This is the *slow train* to London.

Adverbs usually go with verbs:
'Good night,' she *said quietly*.
He *went slowly* up the steps to his house.

To form adverbs, we often add *-ly* to an adjective:
quick → quickly   polite → politely
careful → carefully   noisy → noisily
Note: good → well   fast → fast

Could you …?

We use *Could you …?* to ask people to do things

Could you	open the window? buy me a newspaper?	Yes, of course. No, sorry.

Verb + preposition

listen to	I never watch TV, but I *listen to* the radio.
talk to	I often *talk to* people at the bus stop.
look at	*Look at* me! I can swim!
arrive at	The train *arrives at* the station at 6.00.
think about	What's the answer? I must *think about* it.
talk about	He always *talks about* the weather.

21   Good, better, best

Comparative adjectives

Short adjectives (one or two syllables): add -er.
Long adjectives: use more + adjective.

The Pyramids are *older* than the Acropolis.

A Porsche is *more expensive* than a VW Golf.

Superlatives

Short adjectives: add -est.
Long adjectives: use the *most* + adjective.

The biggest diamond
in the world: the
'Golden Jubilee'

The most expensive
diamond in the world:
the 'D Flawless'

Comparative and superlative forms

rich	richer	richest
cheap	cheaper	cheapest
clean	cleaner	cleanest
safe	safer	safest
big	bigger	biggest
friendly	friendlier	friendliest
beautiful	more beautiful	most beautiful
dangerous	more dangerous	most dangerous
expensive	more expensive	most expensive
good	better	best

Other useful vocabulary

agree   difficult   use (v.)   disagree   actor

22   Free time

Leisure activities

go for + noun

go for	a walk a drive a bike ride	go for	a drink a meal a picnic

go to + noun

go to	the cinema a concert a party

go + -ing

go	shopping swimming skiing

Other verbs

do	an outdoor sport an indoor sport	play	football cards	visit	friends relatives

Sports and activities

football   basketball   volleyball   tennis   table tennis

walking   running   climbing   skiing   windsurfing

like, enjoy + -ing

After *like* and *enjoy*, we can use a noun or an -ing form:

I like nice clothes.   I enjoy football.
I like shopping.   I enjoy watching football.

I don't like card games.
I don't like playing cards.

Other useful vocabulary

a bike ride   lose weight   physical exercise
sports event   spend money

Study pages K

Verb + to

After *want*, *need*, *would like*, we can use a noun or
to + infinitive:

I want I need I'd like	a new bike.	I want I need I'd like	to buy a new bike. to go home now.

Questions:

Do you want Do you need Would you like	a new bike? to buy a new bike? to go home now?

Expressions with *go*

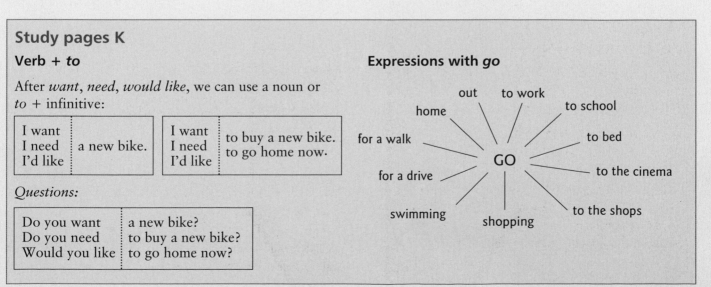

out   to work
home   to school
for a walk   to bed
GO
for a drive   to the cinema
swimming   shopping   to the shops

23 Future plans

going to

To talk about intentions or plans in the future, we use *going to*.

I'm going to He's/She's going to We're going to They're going to	stay with friends.

Questions

Are you going to write to her? Is she going to buy a flat? What are you going to do? When is he going to visit us?

Present continuous

To talk about things in the near future that are *already arranged*, we use the Present continuous:

My aunt and uncle *are staying* with us next week.
We*'re going* to the cinema this evening.
I*'m playing* tennis tomorrow afternoon.

Future time expressions

this

I'm going to watch TV *this evening*.
What are you doing *this afternoon*?

next

My brother's coming to stay *next week*
We're going to go skiing *next January*.

tomorrow

What are you doing *tomorrow*?
I'm going to work *tomorrow evening*.

Useful vocabulary

plan (v.)	move (v.)	late
exactly	housework	

24 Feelings

I'm hungry, etc.

I'm I feel	hungry. thirsty. tired. ill. hot. cold .

I'm hungry = I want to eat.
I'm thirsty = I want to drink.
I'm tired = I want to have a rest.

Feelings

happy    sad    upset    angry

excited    surprised    frightened

Present tense: I feel so happy!
He's very upset about it.

Past tense: I was so excited, I didn't sleep all night.
We felt really angry about it.

Reactions

I	enjoyed didn't enjoy	the film.

It was	interesting. boring. funny. sad.

Suggestions

Why don't you have a rest?
Shall I call a doctor?
Let's watch a video.

Other useful vocabulary

laugh	invite	hold (held)

Irregular verbs

Infinitive	Past tense
be	was/were
bring	brought
build	built
buy	bought
can	could
catch	caught
come	came
cost	cost
do	did
drink	drank
drive	drove
eat	ate
fall	fell
feel	felt
find	found
fly	flew
get	got
give	gave
go	went
have	had
keep	kept
know	knew
leave	left
lose	lost
make	made
pay	paid
put	put
read	read /red/
ride	rode
run	ran
say	said
see	saw
sell	sold
send	sent
sing	sang
sit	sat
sleep	slept
speak	spoke
spend	spent
stand	stood
swim	swam
take	took
tell	told
think	thought
throw	threw
wake	woke
wear	wore
win	won
write	wrote

Phonetic symbols

Vowels

Symbol	Example
/iː/	tree /triː/
/i/	many /ˈmeni/
/ɪ/	six /sɪks/
/e/	bed /bed/
/æ/	black /blæk/
/ʌ/	much /mʌtʃ/
/ɑː/	car /kɑː/
/ɒ/	hot /hɒt/
/ɔː/	sport /spɔːt/
/ʊ/	look /lʊk/
/uː/	spoon /spuːn/
/ɜː/	girl /gɜːl/
/ə/	about /əˈbaʊt/
	water /ˈwɔːtə/
/eɪ/	play /pleɪ/
/aɪ/	time /taɪm/
/ɔɪ/	boy /bɔɪ/
/əʊ/	home /həʊm/
/aʊ/	out /aʊt/
/ɪə/	here /hɪə/
/eə/	there /ðeə/

Consonants

Symbol	Example
/p/	pen /pen/
/b/	book /bʊk/
/t/	take /teɪk/
/d/	dog /dɒg/
/k/	cat /kæt/
/g/	go /gəʊ/
/tʃ/	church /tʃɜːtʃ/
/dʒ/	jumper /ˈdʒʌmpə/
/f/	for /fɔː/
/v/	love /lʌv/
/θ/	think /θɪŋk/
/ð/	this /ðɪs/
/s/	six /sɪks/
/z/	is /ɪz/
/ʃ/	shop /ʃɒp/
/ʒ/	leisure /ˈleʒə/
/h/	house /haʊs/
/m/	make /meɪk/
/n/	name /neɪm/
/ŋ/	bring /brɪŋ/
/l/	look /lʊk/
/r/	road /rəʊd/
/j/	young /jʌŋ/
/w/	wear /weə/

Stress

Dictionaries usually show stress by a mark (/ˈ/) before the stressed syllable: teacher /ˈtiːtʃə/; about /əˈbaʊt/; America /əˈmerɪkə/.

Acknowledgements

The authors would like to thank the following for their contributions to *Language in Use Beginner*:

- for contributing to the recorded material: Mohammed Bakali, Richard Chan, Sean Connolly, Dawn Coutts, Natasha Doff, Hazel Jones, Henry Jones, Thomas Jones, Alessandra Salvalajo, André Zaharias, Gabriella Zaharias.
- for research into reading material: Sean Connolly.
- for providing data for the Unit 7 questionnaire: students and teachers at the Bell Language School, Anglia Polytechnic University, Newnham Language Centre and EF International School, Cambridge.
- for designing the course: James Arnold and Stephanie White (Gecko Ltd).
- for commissioning artwork: Wendy Homer (Gecko Ltd).
- for commissioning photographs: Karen Homer (Gecko Ltd).
- for the production of recorded material: Martin Williamson (Prolingua Productions) and Peter and Diana Thompson (Studio AVP).
- for picture research: Sandie Huskinson-Rolfe of PHOTOSEEKERS.
- for help in producing the Pilot edition: Victoria Adams.
- for illustrations in the Pilot edition: Tania Lewis.

The authors would also like to thank the following at Cambridge University Press:

- Colin Hayes for his continuing support and help.
- Peter Donovan for organising the project.
- Jo Barker for overseeing the design of the course.
- Linda Matthews for control of production.
- Sue Wiseman and Val Grove for general administrative help.
- all CUP staff for arranging piloting and the following for providing feedback: Stephanie Collins, Kate Cory-Wright, Lindsay Kelly.

Special thanks go to:

- James Dingle of Cambridge University Press, for his expert management of the various stages of the project, and his close involvement with the development of Beginner level.
- Meredith Levy, our editor, for her professionalism, good judgement and tireless attention to detail.

The authors and publishers would like to thank the following individuals and institutions for their help in commenting on the material and for the invaluable feedback which they provided:

Silvia Ronchetti, ISP, en lenguas Vivas Juan R. Fernández, Buenos Aires, Argentina; Maria Edvirgem Zeny, Sociedade Brasileira de Cultura Inglesa, Curitiba, Brazil; Marketa Kozerova, The Bell School, Prague, Czech Republic; Duncan Lambe, Mr Diab and Mr Azzam, British Council Teaching Centre, Giza, Egypt; Jennifer Tavassoli, Gif sur Yvette, France; Susanna Magnani, ITC Rosa Luxembourg, Bologna, Italy; Cinzia Riguzzi and Sonia Selleri, Bologna, Italy; Nicolo Arcadipane, International House, Livorno, Italy; Sharon Hartle, Verona, Italy; Paul Lewis, Aichi Shukutoku Junior College, Nagoya, Japan; Akishi Kimura, Kato Gakuen Gyoshu Koko, Numazu, Japan; Zofia Riesinger, Prywatne LO, "University II", Chorzow, Poland; Magda Moran, English Unlimited, Gdańsk, Poland; Anna Sikorzyńska, Warsaw, Poland; Heather Meachem, Cambridge School, Lisbon, Portugal; Helen Engel, Lomonosov State University, Moscow, Russia; Brian Brennan, International House, Barcelona, Spain; Peter Myring, Merit School, Barcelona, Spain; Liz Bitterli, Kaufmannische Berufschule, Uster, Switzerland; Rodney Moore and Terence Broomfield, Dream Development Centre, Bangkok, Thailand; Andrew Coyle, Australia Centre, Chiang Mai, Thailand; Vahide Tümleayan and Zehra Gurtin, Özel Bornova Koleji, Izmir, Turkey; Anita Akkas, Middle East Technical University, Ankara, Turkey; Pauline Desch, Brasshouse Centre, Birmingham, UK; John Kay, ITTC, Bournemouth, UK.

The authors and publishers are grateful to the following copyright owners for permission to reproduce copyright material:

Dick James Music Ltd © 1967 for the extract from 'Love is all around', written by Reg Presley, lyrics reproduced by kind permission of the publisher, lyrics reproduced for the European Union (excluding Italy, Sweden and Denmark) by kind permission of Music Sales Ltd; Josephine Jones for the poem 'Friends' on p. 33.

The authors and publishers are grateful to the following illustrators, photographers and photographic sources:

Illustrators: Gerry Ball: pp. 29 *ml*, 53 *m*; Chris Brown: pp. 9 *tr*, 44 *t*, 96, 104 *t*; Paul Davies: p. 83 *t*; Rachel Deacon: pp. 8 *t*, 8 *m*, 19 *t*, 33, 34, 48 *t*, 81 *t*; Karen Donnelly: pp. 84, 108 *b*, 115, 116, 117, 118, 119, 120, 121, 123, 124, 125; Nick Duffy: pp. 10, 20 *tr*, 26 *m*, 48 *b*, 54 *tl*, 55, 70 *b*, 76 *t*, 87 *l*, 92 *t*, 97 *b*, 102 *b*; Phil Healey: pp. 8 *b*, 17 *m*, 29 *mr*, 31 *l*, 40, 47 *m*, 49 *m*, 57, 63 *bl*, 93, 103 (F); Rosalind Hudson: pp. 11, 52 *b*, 60, 64, 95 *l*,

103 (B); Nadime James: pp. 16 *b*, 17 *t*, 25 *t*, 31 *mr*; Mark McLaughlin: pp. 30 *l*, 43, 65, 67, 86 *l*; Amanda McPhail: p. 91; David Mitcheson: p. 106 *b*; Des Nicholas: pp. 20 *m*, 25 *t*, 31 *br*, 35 *t*, 56, 71 *m*, 106 *t*, 107, 108 *t*; Mark Olyrold: p. 52 *m*; Pantelis Palios: pp. 36 *mb*, 38 *ml*, 49 *b*, 54 *ml*, 62 *t*, 79 *tl*, 99 *b*, 103 (D); Jeff Parker: pp. 39 *mr*, 42 *m*, 90 *m*; Tracy Rich: pp. 14 *bl*, 28 *t*, 45 *t*, 51 *t*, 52 *m*, 54 *br*, 58, 69, 71 *t*; Rachel Ross: p. 102 *t*; James Sneddon: pp. 11 *b*, 12 *t*, 13 *m*, 15, 18, 19 *mb*, 22, 25 *b*, 27 *t*, 28 *b*, 32, 38, 39 *t*, 39 *b*, 42 *t*, 44 *m*, 44 *b*, 46 *b*, 47 *t*, 47 *b*, 53 *b*, 63 *br*, 67 *mr*, 75, 76 *b*, 77, 79 *tr*, 82, 83 *b*, 90 *t*, 92 *m*, 95 *r*, 101 *b*, 103 (J), 105, 106 *m*, 108 *m*, 109, 115 *bl*, 116 *t*, 118 *b*, 122; Holly Swain: pp. 50, 99 *t*; Kath Walker: pp. 9 *tl*, 14 *br*, 16 *t*, 30 *r*, 41 *b*, 54 *l*, 62 *b*, 70 *m*, 78, 86 *b*, 94.

Photographic sources: Adams Picture Library: pp. 17 *bl*, 105 *tl*, *tc*; Allsport/Chris Cole: p. 9 (D), Allsport/David Rogers: p. 9 (E); Art Directors and TRIP Photo Library: pp. 29 *bl*, 103 (L), Art Directors/TRIP/T Schwarz: p. 88 *l*; Gavin Hellier/Aspect Picture Library: pp. 17 *bc*, 61 (A), Derek Bayes/Aspect: p. 104 *br*; Biofotos Associates: p. 21 *mc*; *Wheatfield with Cypresses*, 1889 (oil on canvas), by Vincent Van Gogh (1853–90), National Gallery/Bridgeman Art Library, London/New York: pp. 19 *bc*, 105 *m*; *The Thinker* (*Le Penseur*) (bronze), by Auguste Rodin (1840–1917), Private Collection/Bridgeman: p. 73; *Joan of Arc at the Coronation of King Charles VII 1422*, 1854, by Jean Auguste Dominique Ingres (1780–1867), Louvre, Paris/Peter Willi/Bridgeman: p. 87 *cr*; Britstock/Bernd Ducke: p. 61 (D & G); R. Ellis/Camera Press London: p. 104 *tr*, John Zimmerman/Curtis/Camera Press: p. 72 (1.1) *br*; Canon (UK) Limited: p. 89 *m*; The J. Allan Cash Photolibrary: pp. 25, 103 (A); *Lady in Blue* (painting by numbers line drawing), by Henri Matisse, © Succession H. Matisse/DACS 1999: pp. 19 *bl*, 105 *bl*; James Davis Travel Photography: pp. 68 *m*, 103 (I); Delas Tours, Ithaki: p. 77 *t*, *tc*; Colin Keates, Natural History Museum/Dorling Kindersley: p. 21 *tl*, *tc*, *bcl*; *Unmasking the Face*, by Paul Ekman and Wallace V. Friesen, 1975, © Paul Ekman: p. 101; ET Archive: p. 87 *cl*; Mary Evans Picture Library: p. 87 *l*; Eye Ubiquitous Picture Library/Gavin Wickham: p. 17 *br*, Eye Ubiquitous/Julia Waterlow: pp. 24 *r*, 45 *bc*; Nick Tapsell/Ffotograff: p. 59 *tr*; Getty Images: p. 72 (1.2) *bc*; The Ronald Grant Archive: p. 72 (1.2) *tr*; Sally Greenhill: p. 105 *tcl*; Robert Harding Picture Library: pp. 59 *bl*, *br*, 80; David Hockney, *A Bigger Splash*, 1967 (acrylic on canvas, 96" × 96") © David Hockney: pp. 19 *br*, 105 *br*; Michael Holford/V & A Museum: p. 21 *br*; Nick Hadfield/The Hutchison Library: p. 104 *bc*; The Image Bank/David Vance: p. 105 *tr*; Images Colour Library: p. 13 *tl*; CFCL/Image Select: pp. 59 *tl*, 81 *tr*; Roger Scruton/Impact Photos: p. 81 *bl*; Chris Jones: p. 77 *bc*; Carolco (Courtesy Kobal): p 40 *l*, RKO (Courtesy Kobal): p. 17 *tl*, Universal (Courtesy Kobal): p. 72 *ml*; London Features International: p. 53 *tl*; 'Courtesy of McDonald's Restaurants Limited': p. 40 *r*; Bossemeyer/Bilderberg/Network: p. 45 *br*; Tayacan/Panos Pictures: p. 24 *bl*, Gregory Wrone/Panos: p. 45 *bl*; The Photographers' Library: p. 89 *b*; Photostage/Donald Cooper: p. 72 (1.2) *br*; Pictor International: pp. 51 *tr*, *bl*, 72 (1.1) *tr*, 104 *tl*; Pictures Colour Library/Clive Sawyer: p. 61 (B); Popperfoto/Anthony Bolante: p. 29 *br*, Popperfoto: p. 87 *m*, *br*; PowerStock/Zefa: pp. 14 *tcr*, *tr*, Powerstock/Zefa/Charles Tyler: p. 61 (F); Redferns Music Picture Library/Mick Hutson: p. 9 *bc*, Redferns/Des Willie: p. 9 *br*, Redferns/Tim Hall: p. 17 *tc*, Redferns/RB: p. 53 *cr*/RB; Rex Features Limited/Sipa: p. 9 (B), Rex/Tim Rooke: p. 17 *tr*, 29 *tl*, Rex/Boulat/Jobard: p. 29 *tr*, Rex/Brian Rasic: p. 53 *bl*; Vaughan Fleming/Science Photo Library: p. 21 *ml*; Scotland in Focus/D. Torrance: p. 24 *tl*; Jules Selmes: pp. 12 *b*, 20 *tl*, 20 *tl*, 27 *m*, 35 *b*, 36 *t*, 37 *b*, 41 *t*, 45 *m*, 46 *m*, 49 *t*, 97 *m*, 98 *t*, 100, 103 (C & G); Spectrum Colour Library: p. 85 background; Sporting Pictures (UK) Limited: pp. 9 (F), 85 inset, 103 (K), 104 *tc*; The Stockmarket: p. 61 (C); Tony Stone Images/Martin Rogers: p. 21 *tr*, TSI/Tony Latham: pp. 51 *tl*, 103 (H), TSI/Dale Durfee: p. 51 *bc*, TSI/David Hanover: p. 51 *br*, TSI/Glen Allison: pp. 61 (E), 103 (E), TSI/Neil Beer: p. 68 *b*, TSI/Cosmo Condina: p. 88 *r*, TSI/Richard Passmore: p. 96, TSI/Stephen Studd: p. 104 *bl*; Ann Suter: p. 77 *b*; SuperStock/Musée du Louvre, Paris: p. 72 (1.1)*tl*; Tempsport/S. Ruet/Sygma: p. 9 (A), Tempsport/T. Orbant/Sygma: p. 9 (C), Micheline Pelletier/Sygma: p. 9 *bl*; Telegraph Colour Library/Antonio Mo: pp. 14 *tcl*, TCL/Spencer Rowell: p. 32, TCL/Gavin Hellier: p. 68 *t*, TCL/Benelux Press: p. 81 *br*; Press Association/Topham: p. 72 (1.2) *tl*, Topham Picturepoint: p. 72 (1.2) *bl*; Courtesy of the Topkapi Palace Museum, Turkey: p. 21 *bl*; Janine Wiedel: p. 105 *tm*; Kyocera Yashica (UK) Limited: p. 89 *t*.

t = top m = middle b = bottom r = right l = left c = centre

Picture Research by Sandie Huskinson-Rolfe of PHOTOSEEKERS.
Cover design by Dunne & Scully.
Design, production, colour scanning and reproduction handled by Gecko Limited, Bicester, Oxon.
Sound recordings by Martin Williamson, Prolingua Productions at Studio AVP.
Freelance editorial work by Meredith Levy.